WILL
YOU BE
HERE
WHEN I
GET
HOME?

WILL YOU BE HERE WHEN I GET HOME?

CLAIRE CASHIN

MERCIER PRESS

WHAT YOU NEED TO READ

MERCIER PRESS

Douglas Village, Cork

www.mercierpress.ie

Trade enquiries to Columba Mercier Distribution,

55a Spruce Avenue, Stillorgan Industrial Park, Blackrock, Dublin

© Claire Cashin, 2006

Cover illustration by Marguerite Kiely

ISBN: 1 85635 521 7 and 978 1 85635 521 6

10 9 8 7 6 5 4 3 2 1

A CIP record for this title is available from the British Library

Mercier Press receives financial assistance from
the Arts Council/An Chomhairle Ealaíon

Printed and bound in Ireland by Colur Books Ltd

CONTENTS

'It is not because things are difficult that we do not dare;
it is because we do not dare that they are difficult.'

— Seneca

*My sincere thanks to Declan Hassett
– the man who made me dare!*

*For everyone in my life who loves me,
I have you all to thank for my sanity and my
ability to love, forgive and laugh at myself.
This is especially for my family – and for Mai.*

PREFACE

I'm not a literary person, nor do I have a special eloquence or gift for beautiful words or prose. Like most people, I guess, I have a story to tell. Some may like it. Others may not. Not everyone in life will agree with your opinion, but for me, this had to be written. It has helped me. I am an adopted person. That sounds very dramatic, but it's not really. It's just a part of who I am, the cards I was dealt. I wouldn't change a thing in my life, really, because I am who I am today because of what I have learned. In life, I have tried to help others where I can, and if by writing this I am able to help just one person, then I have done what I set out to do.

I grew up in Cork with Colum, Eileen and Mary and they are my family. As time passed and adolescence hit, I began to wonder about what being adopted meant and eventually, with help, I realised that I needed to go looking for what people called 'my birth mother'. I found a lot more than I bargained for, a roller-coaster of emotions and a family unit 100 per cent mine by blood! This story tells of what happened, and it is written for anyone with an interest in this subject or for those who need help in trying to understand the feelings that haunt them. It's for those who are adopted or for the family network that tries to help them understand.

I do not wish this book to read like an angry, bitter accusation, and more than anything I have tried to open up and let people inside, to see the very real and raw emotions at each stage during this journey – not only to see them but, hopefully, to be able to learn from my mistakes.

Someone dear to me recently said, 'Everyone loves a happy story.' This *is* a happy story and one that I believe to be, although not quite unique, unusual all the same. It contains many memories, some very painful, in which I doubted my very being, but most of them happy and hopeful. The need to write this, however, stems from something deep within me. I wrote this for a reason. When I began my search to find my birth mother, I had no real hopes of finding her and, to some extent, I had set myself up for a fall. But as time continued, I began to allow myself to accept my feelings and not to deny them any more. I was not prepared, however, for the force of the raw emotions that began to sit heavily on my heart.

It's very easy to look back and smile, realising now what my heart was vainly trying to tell me in my younger years. When you have accepted the past and can look to the future with a smile, it's hard to understand why things seemed so difficult all those years ago. I know now that, apart from the precious love and support I received from my family, above all what I needed was to know that my feelings were not frowned upon and were accepted. I needed acknowledgement that my feelings were normal. Moreover, I needed to learn from others in similar situations – how they dealt with their anger, their grief, their happiness, their fear and every other emotion that coursed through me.

I searched for books and information on the internet, in book stores and any other medium I could think of. I found support books for those who wished to adopt a child and advice about the problems they might expect as the child grew older. I found books by parents who had already adopted a child, describing very clinically what happened, why and what to do about it. I found books advising the best way to approach the actual adoption and everything to do with an adoptee's teenage years. Most of the information available dealt with how to raise an adopted child or how to cope with personality traits that may manifest during the teenage years. There was *nothing*, it seemed, written for the adoptee, advising how to carry out a search for birth parents, how to understand your feelings once information had been gained and, above all, how to take steps forward in trying to forge relationships with people in your life, some of whom were in fact your own flesh and blood.

For the reader, at times during this book it might seem like common sense to simply have grabbed at every opportunity and taken a chance. What have you got to lose, right? I love my family very much, yet have always longed to ask a simple question: why? Why was I given up for adoption? It's a question that I firmly believe each adopted person asks at some stage during their lives, and one that deserves an answer. It's not just the search for birth parents that is difficult, but the real fear that by starting this search you might hurt those you love or leave yourself open to heartache. It might sound melodramatic, but it is a battle that rages inside you day in and day out. I needed to ask the woman who gave birth to me why I was given up for adoption. I also worried about the hurt that I could cause my Mum, Dad and sister. My family loved me with every breath in their bodies, and I could not have carried on the search without their blessing, love, support and understanding. As time passed, I began to really appreciate how loving and understanding they really were.

I started my search in 1995 and I can say, with my hand on my heart, it has been both the hardest and one of the most rewarding experiences of my life. What I learned during these years has given me more understanding of myself. Most precious of all is the gift to be able to accept myself for what I am, which has been a long time coming. Too long. As I write this, I feel tears gathering, but they are tears now of thanks and joy. My dad always said my eyes were very close to my bladder. He's probably right … he knows me better than I know myself at times.

This book is not meant to be a literary masterpiece, nor a cure for what ails you. It is simply the story of what I learned and, most of all, how one person can't possibly go it alone. If you have faith, love and friendship in your life, you are truly blessed and anything is possible.

Life has its ups and downs but, boy, when it's good, stick a smile on your face and enjoy every minute of it. Ray Murphy, a great family friend, used to say at these times 'If I was any better I'd be boasting!'

1

ADOPTION *IS* DIFFERENT

I am thirty-two years of age and an adopted person. If someone had told me a few years back that I might write a book, really, I would have laughed at such an idiotic idea. Just the thought of revealing private and personal thoughts about mistakes I have made and about my life would have been anathema to me. Today, however, my priorities have changed, and the bigger picture is far more important to me – the chance to share what I can and try to offer an insight into what being adopted has meant for me.

I was adopted by Colum, Eileen and Mary. I cannot say simply that Mum and Dad alone adopted me, for Mary was ten by the time I became a part of their family, and as the years passed she mothered me as much as Eileen did. Some facts to build a picture about my life: I work as a receptionist in Mallow, I have been married to Aidan for the past seven years and live a very normal life, cooking dinners, doing the washing and walking the dogs of an evening, with a few vodka and Diet Cokes thrown in for good measure!

This part of the book, however, is not about what it is I do to earn a living. Neither does it concern the people in my life, for there will be time enough to meet them later. It is about being adopted and what I have learned.

I am essentially a good person. I have *learned* that I have many strengths: I am caring, loving and giving, considerate, hard working and I have a good sense of humour. I have also learned that I have many faults: I can be too sensitive; I hurt far too easily; I have a fiery temper and have little patience at times. I use the word 'learned' because it is only of late that I can accept my faults and, more importantly, accept and be proud of my strengths. I can be proud of myself and realise that, while I am far from perfect, I'm not that bad a person. I now have the confidence to face myself in the mirror and smile. Twelve years ago I was self-conscious, untrusting, self-doubting, confrontational, unforgiving and angry at the world and everyone in it. I had to be able to control my own little world – what I did, whom I saw, what we talked about, how I did my job, how quickly relationships developed – and God forbid that you asked me to leave these self-imposed boundaries!

Now I have the ability to bend a little, and I don't have to rely on being able to control everything. When younger, I reasoned that if everything in my life was predetermined, set and planned for in some fashion, then I was able to plan my reactions to everything, and in this way I believed that nothing could catch me unawares. I was able to plan my emotions to some extent and thus maintain the person I wanted the world to see. I certainly did not want anyone, not even my family, to see the terrified little girl who began to 'understand' that my first mummy gave me away because there must have been something wrong with me. As a young child and teenager, I feared that it was only a matter of time before others realised this as well …

I have lived much of my life differently because I am an adopted person. When I first started to write about adoption in an effort to understand myself, I did not wish to write an in-depth examination of the psyche of adopted people. I really did not want my story to be that serious. Adoption is a serious matter, however, and as I struggled to explain how I felt at different stages of my life, I realised that in order for the families and loved ones of any person who is adopted to understand, it is important to explain how being adopted can affect your life, how misconceptions and mistruths can root themselves in your mind and heart and can shape your understanding of yourself.

It is only now, having had the courage to look deep inside, that I can talk openly about what I have learned about myself. When I was younger I made myself believe that I was no different to any other child in the world. But being an adopted child *is* different. Now I laugh with the realisation that, of course, every one of us is different from the person next to us – that's what makes life so wonderful. But when younger I needed so badly to be the same as every other child. The difference I began to feel as a child, however, stemmed from something far greater than having curly hair or straight hair, or being thin or chubby. This difference stemmed from having two mummies but one of them 'gave me away'.

It has taken me thirty years to realise that my bedtime story merely cushioned the realisation that I was, possibly, very different from other 'natural' children. That's another useless choice of word … 'natural' … was I abnormal or unnatural in some way? Is it *only* natural for mothers who actually carry a child and give birth to a child to love them as their own? Is it not natural to love a child just as much, if not more in some circumstances, when you did *not* carry this child in your womb for nine months? What's so unnatural about a woman loving a child that they did not give birth to? There are no natural or unnatural children or parents. There should be just the love for a child when it becomes part of a family. I refer to this because, in my opinion, a stigma seems to be still attached to adoption and adopted people.

The truth of the matter is that many adopted kids *do* feel different to other children. Not only was I conceived within another woman's womb, but also the relationship that developed between my family and myself was very different to that of many other children and their family members. An adopted person can, in fact, interact with the world in a different way, whether because of its first few weeks without the ability to forge a bond with its mother or because they learn, a little too late in my opinion, that they are different. We may be special or chosen and loved by our parents and family, but we need more of an explanation when growing up.

Think of a baby that spends its first few weeks of life in an adoption agency. It surely can't be good for a baby to lie, for the most part, on its own in a cot, being tended to merely when hungry or in need of changing. I know four other adopted people very well and, although every case is certainly not the same, we all were with an adoption society for a minimum of six weeks before joining our families. I am no expert on child psychology, but I do have serious questions concerning the effect this may have on a child. My mother and father received a telephone call shortly after I was born to tell them that they had a new daughter. What took so long that I could not be collected sooner than nearly two months later? When I joined my new family, I then gradually learned that, while I was surely loved by all family members, a woman out there somewhere gave me away, as I understood it, for reasons unknown. This can affect each person differently as they grow and learn about forging relationships with others.

Consider the relationships we might be lucky enough to have in our lives, for example with colleagues, friends, family members, school or college buddies, boyfriends/girlfriends and so on. Imagine all the gifts we can bestow on these people – the gifts of love, trust, laughter, camaraderie, intimacy, friendship … The list really is endless. Now try and understand how crippling it might be to grow into adulthood distrusting most people outside the family unit, because your first mum gave you away and as a result you cannot trust people. After all, this was the woman who should have loved me from the first moment she saw me, and if I could not trust her, then whom could I trust? As a result, try and imagine being unwilling to let down your defences for fear of getting hurt, while at the same time hiding behind what might be viewed as an outgoing, fun and game-for-a-laugh persona. I think, to some extent, that may be how I lived my younger years, afraid to admit many truths, unaware to a large extent of some of my innermost feelings.

I believe that a child that is born to its parents, with the gift of growing up secure in their love and the knowledge that they were wanted from the very moment of conception, reacts to the world differently to a child who is adopted. If you know you are adopted, although you might have the intelligence to know that, yes, you are loved by your family, still, at the back of your mind, you know that this first mum relinquished you and gave the right to love you to someone else. You know that she might have done this to offer you a chance at a better life, but it doesn't make you *feel* any better. I know my family believed I was the same as any one of them because I was loved just as much, but in many ways it's like being told that you're not fat, you're cuddly. This information might be accepted easily by a child, but one day the child grows up, looks in the mirror and realises that, in fact, the reality is very different. You are more than a little bit cuddly!

It's important to be told right from the start that you are adopted, that you are loved and accepted as one of the family, but that adoption *is* different from the usual way in which children become members of any family. I knew I was adopted, but as a very young child I never really heard much detail or information about this other mummy apart from the fact that she existed, some-where. The lack of talk about this other mummy seemed to suggest to me that it was not good to ask questions about her or to want to know anything about being adopted. After all, if she was not spoken about by my family, then I in turn must not speak of her. Mum has always held the very strong opinion that they should have been told the circumstances surrounding my adoption and about my birth mum – not necessarily her name or whereabouts, but certainly the facts surrounding my conception, what sort of woman she was, her medical history and so on.

As a young child you learn from your family and begin to understand your world and your place in it. That I was the same as Mary, my sister, was the foundation of my understanding of my place at home. I reacted to the world the same way as Mary because in younger years this was simply my family, without a need to examine where we all came from. As I grew older however and started school, I realised the true meaning of being adopted. I had another mummy out there somewhere, and so I had to learn the skills necessary to function in this newly perceived world.

I was a wilful child and could not stand to be bullied or told what to do, preferring to make my own decision, right or wrong. I believed, incorrectly, that if I was a good girl, I would be worthy of love. Everyone loves a good girl, don't they? I fought anyone who tried to take the ability to make my own decisions from me like a wild cat. This oppositional behaviour manifested itself in our home, in me, each time a routine was changed or something was forced upon me. I especially needed to fight my corner where Mary was concerned as if it were a matter of life and death. This is probably one of the main reasons Mary and I fought a lot as children.

I suppose it goes back to my self-protection mechanism. Be strong; be self-reliant; don't lean on others because they may hurt you. It's a philosophy that has left me in hot water at times and I have learned that, instead of accepting me at face value, people tend to view me as stand-offish and cold in many ways. But that's entirely up to them. If someone cares enough about me, they will take the time to see what lies behind the tough exterior. For people who know me and accept me as I am, idiosyncrasies and all, they can accept that I simply take a lot of time to allow people in and let my guard down. Those who know me can see the good in me also. I have many true friends who have been at my side through thick and thin.

As I grew up thoughts of this other mother crept into my heart. As a teenager, I began to think more about my birth mother and the fact that she actually gave me away, her own flesh and blood. So, even though my family considered me to be no different, I knew I was! Trying to reconcile my family's belief with my own feelings and the need to find some answers began to weigh heavily on my shoulders. I was torn in two, I loved my family and wanted to protect them from all that was welling up inside me and in particular the need to know why I was adopted. During my teenage years, on occasion, when I had a few drinks inside me, an angry little bitch found her way out each and every time. Angry at the world, angry at my birth mother, angry perhaps even at Mum and Dad … who knows?

It can't be easy to teach your child to never be afraid to reach for the stars and, if you don't get there, not to be too disappointed – there is always tomorrow. Mum and Dad were able to give me that, which is no mean achievement, considering I was asking myself some fairly serious questions as I grew up. I began to question whether Mary ever wished she had another sister. I believed that I was lucky to find Colum, Eileen and Mary because, really, if I had not found them, I would probably be on my own, as I thought myself not really good enough to be loved. They lost a little girl the year after Mary was born, and it seemed to me that, as a younger child, I was second best for them. Surely they would have preferred to have loved their 'real' daughter? The mind of a child can be so delicate, and now I can see the madness of believing that, but it was the reality for me at that age.

My relationship with my family has seen moments of anger

and bitterness, though few and far between. When you have the dynamics of more than two people in any home, there are bound to be fireworks sometimes. It took many years before I trusted the permanence of our family unit at home. As a child, I was homesick when I went to Irish college. I was terribly homesick when I travelled abroad for a few years. Home was the one place in my life where I felt secure. I can almost hear you thinking – 'What's so different about you feeling this way from any other child? Many kids feel homesickness and are clingy when growing up!' But I believed that I was not worthy of love, not really, because of this first mother and what I understood as her rejection of me. The mother who gave birth to you was meant to be the one person who *really* loved you and would protect you and be there for you. But she didn't want me.

My family finally managed to teach me, despite my inability to completely accept the fact that I was worthy of love and deserved to be respected. As Nana, Mum's mother, always said, 'The value that you place on yourself, is the value that others place on you.' My family gave me refuge and made me safe. But the true meaning of adoption began to haunt me – why did this first mum give me away? Though I tried to deny these feelings for many years, they manifested themselves at every opportunity as I reached my late teens.

I was adopted as a baby and have experienced some doubts and learned some things about myself that I'm not so proud of, but that's not terribly unique. We've all had different lessons in life and each of them forms our character in some way. I have been lucky enough, so far, to have escaped heartache to the degree much of my family and extended family have suffered. It's what keeps me grounded at times. I am writing about how adoption hurt, really badly, in years past, but there are always others in life that are far worse off than you. What's important is your attitude to whatever knocks you are dealt. Being adopted is a state of mind. I spent years fighting it and denying much of my doubts and fears as they ate away at me. I felt great shame, as I believed in earlier years that I was damaged goods, not good enough to be kept by my birth mother. I learned eventually that I had no reason to feel ashamed of who I was, an adopted person, for that shame merely led me to believe that I was not worthy of love and of so many gifts in life. The only thing I can say is that I have been blessed now with many people who care for me deeply. There came a time when I was no longer willing to be the one crying at a party because I felt a great wrong had been done to me.

This book is not only penned for anyone with an interest, for one reason or another, in adoption, it's also written for my famil*ies*, for without them I'd be a different person. I now have two families, and this story is about finding the second one. As people grow older, everyone clings to something, whether it's faith in yourself, God or family or a trust that what will be, will be. Whatever your secret, I believe in God and have faith that we have a life to lead, already set down to some extent, and if we can help others along the way, then that's a life worth living. The French philosopher Voltaire describes it well: 'Every man is guilty of the good job he did not do.' If we can help others, then we should.

So this is my effort to give a little back, to try to help others in my situation and to relieve some pain if I can. If you learn from some of the mistakes I made then I'm happy. Now I can see that regret at what could have been (if I had not been adopted), or for what has been in the past, is really a useless emotion. The time has come for me to forgive my birth mother, the confused, vulnerable and very scared young girl who made the decision to have me adopted. I cannot change the past and I have now let go of the shame and anger. I have begun talking about my feelings with people I love and trust, rather than behaving like a victim.

Eleven years ago I made the decision to search for my birth mother, a decision which would change the rest of my life. But it's not so much the cards you're dealt in life – it's how you play the hand. Life has revealed to me that unthinkably good things can happen regardless!

2

OUT OF THE MOUTHS OF BABES

I was born on 19 March 1974 in Dublin. The name my birth mother had in mind was Jacqueline and she always thought of me as this, I guess. My family, Eileen, Colum and Mary, lived in Cork. The year after Mary was born (1964) their second little girl was stillborn. In the years following this loss, Mary began to ask why she did not have a brother or sister. So ten years after Mary was born, I became a part of the family and was adopted from St Patrick's Guild adoption society in May 1974, aged six weeks old.

When the nun from St. Patrick's visited Colum and Eileen's home before their application to adopt was accepted, she asked whether they wanted a boy or a girl. Mary, aged ten, spoke up and told the nun that she had had a baby sister, but she died. The nun nodded and, I believe, that was that. The next time that my sister and I begin to annoy each other, I might remind her that she only has herself to blame!

I don't know what it feels like to want a baby so badly. Or what it must feel like to apply to adopt, then fill out the paperwork and wait, not knowing if they would be approved, not knowing how long before they would have another baby to love, only to receive a phone call for an appointment, no less, to answer questions about their income, their home, Colum's job and really to answer: what's so good about you? Why should we give you a baby? Mum tells me it seems like they waited forever. Shortly after my birth the phone rang in Beaumont Avenue, and my Dad took the call. He came into the kitchen and told my mum what the nun had told him: 'Your daughter has been born.' I like this story and I believe, and always have done, that God really knew what He was doing in giving me the name Cashin. He knew what that little baby needed and what lay ahead for me. I think in giving us to each other He knew, as a family, we would all be good for each other.

One of the earliest stories I remember being told, and one of my favourites, is of how I 'arrived' in Cork. I don't actually have a recollection or an awareness of finding out that I was adopted. Neither was the stigma of 'being adopted' something that I was aware of, until my later teenage years. Very simply, I just always knew. Mum used tell me, 'You know you didn't grow in Mummy's tummy, but we love you very much.' I grew up with this story. It was my bedtime fairy-tale story. Mum and I had a song we used sing to each other and we'd laugh. Mum would start with, 'Oh you are my …' and I would finish, 'loooovvvvve'. It used send me into fits of laughter, assured of my place in her heart. At such a young age, I was aware, as much as a child can be, of some other tummy somewhere out there, where I had stayed for a while, until I left that tummy and arrived in Cork. Any tummy is as good as the next at that age!

I think my first memory ever was being cradled on their legs and getting we called a 'zerbert' on my tummy. I'm sure we've all administered them at some stage. When you place your lips on someone's tummy and blow so hard your lips reverberate against the skin and make the rudest sound, the louder the better, that's a zerbert! It used send me into fits of laughter and I'd holler, 'Again, again.'

It seemed quite normal to me at this age to grow in someone else's tummy and then to have your mummy and daddy come and collect you in Dublin. After all, Rachael, an old friend, had arrived in Cork the same way. As I grew older, I learned about the postal strike when the signed adoption forms had to be sent back to the adoption agency in Dublin by a certain date. In a panic, Dad and Mum drove up to Dublin from Cork with the letter so that it would make it there on time. That was how much they wanted me. I began to trust, eventually, that they really did love me. Simple little stories like that, making it easy for me to understand, coupled with a lot of love, hugs and zerberts, settled my heart and answered any questions I had at that early age.

I went for a few Sunday drinks with my dad recently on Father's Day, and he told me what a really amazing woman my mum was. He mentioned how he was gone a lot, travelling for work, and how mum was at home all the time with us. We enjoyed our life at home, though, because of how hard Dad worked. He said he hoped Mum knew how much he appreciated what a great mother and wife she was and what an intelligent and loving woman she was. I guess if you haven't told her by now, Dad, I just have.

I was told a story a few years ago about one day when I arrived home from school. I had been asked by our teacher to write a poem or a little story about home or our parents. I wrote some words along the lines of:

My Daddy. My daddy is great fun. We play every Saturday morning and when he's away working, he sometimes brings me surprises when he gets home. He buys me sweeties and brings me to the park. He always makes me laugh. I love my daddy.

For my poor mother, the woman who was present for practically every second of my life, I wrote:

My Mummy. My mummy cooks me dinner!

Like all children, I suppose, I never fully appreciated what a mother's life is like, even though it was mum who was always there to wipe a knee when I fell, or to help me 'make cakes', and she always knew how to make me smile when I was sad. I always had

23

both of them, a mum *and* a dad, who were very present in my life and there was never once when I needed their love that it was not forthcoming. Mum was there for every minute of my life and there are times when I wonder how she ever had the patience to provide such a safe and happy home for us – for me in particular.

Every single day of my younger years, until well into my adolescence, on the way to school, like a broken record, I asked her, 'Mum, will you be here when I get home?' I have since been told that at an even younger age, in playschool, she had to leave her bag with me with a few objects inside it, like her lipstick, because then I knew that she would be coming back for me. Now I ask myself if I really was any different to other children of that age, for many children that are not adopted also cling to their mothers for many years. Even then, however, I think I knew there was something a little bit different about me. Having her bag and lipstick gave me a reassurance that, yes, she would be back for me and, even at playschool age, I had begun to understand that my first mum did not want me and maybe the same thing could happen again. The insecurity was creeping in, but it wasn't until I began school that something happened that was to stay with me for quite a number of years.

I was only about four or five, playing in the avenue one day, while Mary kept a watchful eye on me, when one of my friends, a neighbour at home, said to me, 'Yeah, well, you're adopted anyway'. Now, I doubt if she really knew at her age what she was saying, but kids – they sure can call it like it is. Mary rushed in to Mum, horrified at what had transpired, and Mum just said not to worry about it.

That night, Mum tells me, I sat in the bath and she asked me, 'Did someone say something to you today?' I replied that, yes, this girl had said that I was adopted. Again she told me the 'tummy story' and how much they all loved me. I replied that I knew they

24

loved me and, from the mouths of babes, I added, 'Yeah, well, she's a bitch anyway!' The conversation continued, but looking back I believe that was the first time that being adopted registered a bit more with me and that was the first time that it hurt just a little, that maybe I wasn't quite the same as other kids.

At home, I slowly began to feel secure in the knowledge that my mum and dad wanted me very much and loved me a whole lot, while as the years passed I learned that being adopted meant more than simply growing in another mummy's tummy. It meant that at some stage this other mummy had to have made the decision to give me away. Isn't that such a stupid choice of words? It's a phrase I have always used and, without really thinking about its meaning, it has played on my heart and very being as I grew up. Where did she give me away to and why? As an adult it's easier to rationalise these questions and form answers that make some sense. We can appreciate life's problems and challenges, understand what getting pregnant at an early age must be like, without perhaps the support of family members. But as a child I understood that the words 'given away' meant, for me, that I was not wanted. It was in this frame of mind I learned that maybe I had a lot to make up for. If I was to be loved and accepted, then maybe it would be easier if I tried to become what I believed people wanted me to be.

During my early years at school, at every parent–teacher meeting, my poor mother heard how I was lazy and capable of so much more. What Mum didn't realise is that I had found my calling as the class clown. I was able to make people laugh and as a result I was popular and had lots of friends. I was called in the playground to play games, and as long as I kept being funny I was in no danger of being rejected by my buddies and found to be lacking in something. I was part of them and just like them.

As the years passed and teenage years arrived, along with entrance exams, Intermediate Certificate and Leaving Certificate,

I still revelled in being the class clown and perfected the art, yet realised that, when needed, I would have to pull out the grades to keep Mum and Dad happy. I made good grades at exam time, made people laugh at school and was middle of the road at everything. I did enough to get by yet be accepted by my peers, and just managed to keep any feelings of self-doubt and lack of self-esteem at bay.

As an adult it is much easier to understand the feelings that caused such confusion and hurt as a child and an adolescent. As a child, however, with the lack of insight and ability to communicate your confusion, your innermost fears can develop into beliefs about yourself and your place in your own little world that affect your personality and everyone around you. My best friend was my saviour in my younger years – she still is – someone like me, who understood and *still* understands what I was feeling. We didn't have the answers to some of the questions, but we knew we both felt the same in many ways, which made it all right.

For anyone reading this who is an adopted person, the only thing I can say to you is this. Everything you feel is normal. Every question you feel you need to ask is all right. Above all, be true to yourself and do what your heart tells you to do. Follow with your heart, not your mind. If I had listened to all the sensible reasons I told myself to leave well enough alone, I would never have found myself. Simple as that! My uncle Jim told me once that we will never be given any problem so big that we cannot handle it, and I believe him. It's just a matter of listening to those who love you, accepting a shoulder to lean on sometimes and taking a chance. My parents taught me to have courage and I have them to thank for supporting me on the journey I am about to tell you about.

3

FORGING RELATIONSHIPS

Dad always said that I was a bit of a lunatic as a child, always running around the place, never a moment to be wasted. There were certain times of the year when he might be away mid-week but he was always home by Thursday, and I looked forward to Saturday mornings at home. It was always the same. I'd wake up and go into Mum and Dad's room. Running to the shop for *The Examiner* – before it became known as *The Irish Examiner* – was one of my first jobs on a Saturday morning. Then came play time with Dad, trying to best each other. Inevitably one or the other of us had to admit defeat. I am still proud to say there was an odd occasion when I beat him at his own game. (I discovered the art of pinching under his arm!) Mum was often heard saying as she went down the stairs, 'It will end in tears!' Sometimes it did, but I could still hear the smile in her voice. My memories of earlier years were of parents who were constantly present in my life, always ready with a hug, a kiss or a reassuring word.

It was a happy childhood. Not only were Mary and I blessed with our immediate family, but we were also part of a close-knit family support unit with aunts, uncles and cousins, all with the same love of family and sense of 'divilment' that was present at home. Whenever we met when I was a child, which was often, I remember watching with awe as the songs were sung, the jokes were told and the ball was hopped with such frequency that it was hard to keep up. I have so many memories given to me by each and every aunt, uncle and cousin, far too many to mention, but I owe many of them to the Kielys and to Dad's brothers and sister.

Growing up, I had many buddies but only a few I can call close friends today. There was only one I was always myself with, could laugh or cry with – it didn't seem to matter. Rachael was adopted from St Patrick's Guild also. I used to laugh and call us cot neighbours. I think that without being able to bounce my thoughts and fears off Rachael for so many years, I might have been a very different person. She is truly the only female friend in whom I have ever confided absolutely everything. She is the only person to whom I would dare to reveal everything. I don't have the words that can thank her for that. Maybe it was because Rachael was adopted, maybe not. I like to think we have so much more in common than just being adopted – like *Dirty Dancing*, Michael Jackson and Nutella. The fact is simply this: here was someone who, like myself, despite having a near-perfect upbringing, understood that we were both given away by someone out there for reasons unknown to us.

I never really enjoyed school. As I said, I was the class clown and everyone seemed to like having a laugh with me, and I suppose I viewed that as being accepted by my peers. Through no fault of my friends in school, I always felt isolated from them and have myself to blame. I never admitted to feeling any way other than happy and content. It was easier that way, and in my younger teens it never seemed to bother me. Over the years I became someone who found it easier to try and please others than rock the boat; try and live up to expectations rather than disappoint; try and blend in with the crowd rather than stand out. My distrust of relationships affected my ability to bond with many of my friends in primary school but more especially in secondary school. I began to foster the belief that if I did not let people get to know the real me, they would not be able to reject me or hurt me.

I believed at that age that I owed a great deal to Mum and Dad for giving me such wonderful chances in life. It was around the age of twelve or so that I began to sense from others around me, from society in general, that I had a lot to be thankful for. I was special. My mum and dad came all the way to Dublin for me and gave me a home and family that would love me. I began to wonder what would have happened if no one had collected me – what then? So any feelings that began to surface that possibly could have hurt my family in Cork were suppressed. I believed if I could show them I knew how lucky I was then that would prove my gratitude to them. If I asked questions about this other mum out there somewhere that would be ungrateful of me. I didn't want them to think their love wasn't enough.

Something happened at home around this time that frightened me a lot. On my thirteenth birthday I had a few buddies around for a party. I went into the kitchen and saw Mum and Aunty Marie at the kitchen table and Mum was crying hard. When I asked what was wrong, they tried to laugh and told me to go back in to the party, that nothing was wrong.

A few days later I was told that Dad had cancer and that he had to go into hospital for a few days. The few days turned into a few weeks and I could see from the tears and worried expression on Mum's face every day that something was wrong. I always presumed that I had not appreciated the seriousness of the situation back then, that I was too young. But now I think I did realise that there was a possibility that Dad could die, and this terrified me. I spoke to Rachael recently about how I could not remember much about this time. Because of my close relationship with Dad, she suggested, perhaps I had shut most of these years out of my mind. I think she is right. I have never been able to handle the thought of loss because, up until a few years ago, it made me think about what I perceived as the loss I suffered when I was born, that of my birth mum.

We had planned to go to France on holidays that summer with Mum's sister and her family and I was very excited about that. After Dad's second and third trip into hospital with infections and various problems, it was decided that they would not go to France, but that I could still go with Aunty Marie and her gang. Today I can appreciate that Dad needed time to recuperate and that having a demanding teenager around the house would be difficult. That's normal. But at that age I thought it meant that I needed to be a good girl, not cause trouble and certainly not start asking questions about birth mums and adoption and start crying and causing scenes. Who knows really what goes on in a child's mind? But from the time I came back from France, I shifted into trying not to give expression to my feelings of frustration and confusion. The more I tried to deny these feelings, the more angry and resentful towards everyone I became. It was stupid of me and I really did not give my family the credit they deserved. I guess I was still young and had lessons to learn.

As my early teenage years passed, I could not stop thinking about this birth-mother figure. Dad slowly recovered and I tried to keep any feelings of anger hidden from Mum and Dad, but a rage began to build inside me. I can see now that it was more to do with the fact that I had questions and doubts about myself and why I was adopted rather than actually being given up for adoption. Up until then I had accepted that being adopted was simple. Yes, there was another mum out there who had me adopted, but I was now a Cashin and had grown secure in my place as such.

I began to feel angry about so many things. I was angry at my mum, I think. Maybe I was angry because I believed that I had to keep my feelings of confusion hidden at home. But most of all I was very angry at myself for allowing all these questions into my head. I believed at that time that I had felt fine until I started asking myself all these questions. Why did I have to start now? I really did not understand who or what I was angry at! I lashed out at my sister, who was doing her best to love me. I lashed out at my parents, who were doing their level best to understand me. I lashed out at everyone, really. I believed that everyone put it down to the usual teenage angst and turmoil. Mum, however, recently told me that they knew I was beginning to question why I was adopted. I have wondered since why they did not broach the subject with me and try to talk to me about it. But then Rachael spelled it out for me. She said, 'Maybe they knew that if they pushed you into talking about it, they would push these feelings deeper inside, maybe never to surface again'. It was such a delicate thing and I had to reason it out for myself, when I was good and ready.

Rachael was right. Mum and Dad know me so well that they gave me the time I needed to figure things out for myself, yet at the same time they let me know they would be there for me when I needed them. I tried to suppress all these emotions, yet they began to surface more and more often, despite my best efforts. This was the routine I settled into, and I fought more and more with my parents and with Mary, screaming at them, taking my rage out on them. It was a hard few years for them all, of that I am sure!

I started at Shannon College of Hotel Management, aged seventeen, in 1991, surrounded by people much older and more comfortable in their skin than me, in an environment where you needed to be yourself and know your own voice. I didn't. I found it hard. I went to Brussels in 1992, a young girl with no clue how to survive out of the family home, without the security blanket it had become. I only trusted Mum, Dad and Mary. When I began my own life, I was wary of relationships and would become the person I believed the other person wanted me to be.

At Shannon, while I received a great education, many of the students had already experienced college and had a sense of themselves. The student ethos outside of college hours was very much 'grab a few scoops at the local bar and drink until you drop'. The same as other colleges around the country, I'm sure, but away from home I tried to fall in with this way of living, and I slowly realised that alcohol was no friend when you were trying to keep your true emotions hidden.

I think it slowly became obvious to many around me that there were things I needed to deal with. I remember having what I think were panic attacks, and the simplest problems became huge issues. Any time I went out socially and had too many drinks, 'something' made me terribly upset, but nothing that I seemed able to put into words. I recall one night after work in Brussels, a friend from college, a fellow Corkonian, came to stay for a few days with the gang of us from Shannon who shared a house. We went out, drank until the early hours and I ended up, as was usual, sitting on a windowsill crying bitter tears, ranting incoherently about how life was terrible, yet still unable to articulate that I hated not having the answers to the questions that came unbidden into my mind.

I refused, either drunk or sober, to admit to myself that I had any issues with being adopted or that I needed some answers. In my own mind, I needed nothing from the woman who had me adopted. I was happy as a Cashin, fulfilled and starting my new career in hotel management and I was bloody fine, thank you! That night, for the first time, a college friend from Cork had the courage to say something to me straight up, without mincing his words. He said to me, 'You need to get a grip and find out what it is that's upsetting you, and when you get home, I would suggest you talk to someone, either in your family or find someone professionally. Everything is not all right with you Claire, and it seems as if you can't cope with it alone.' I was appalled at him – how dare he think he knew me so well! But perhaps he knew me well enough and as time passed it became obvious, not only to him, but also to others, that something was causing me pain.

Simply put, I was not happy. I was, in fact, terribly unhappy, but I was unwilling to admit what was wrong. Looking back, maybe I knew inside that I needed answers. But I think I feared that these answers had the ability to inflict more hurt and pain and so I tried to bury my feelings.

In my younger years my self-confidence left a lot to be desired. When considering relationships I had while in Brussels, unknown to myself, I considered it easier to leave someone or hurt someone than to be hurt myself. I had a few boyfriends, but I let no one get close to me. I remember seeing a Dutch student for a few months before leaving Brussels and while we certainly clicked – it was the first time I had real feelings for someone – my most abiding memory from that time was the overwhelming sense of relief when I left Brussels. I was not ready to commit to someone emotionally and things were certainly beginning to get very serious. How could I commit when there was so much turmoil inside? For the next few years I tried to simply concern myself with working hard and trying to enjoy myself.

I think I let myself believe that these feelings might pass, that I'd outgrow them. I was unwilling to accept that maybe I had to look at the connection between being adopted and the way I was feeling at that time. I wouldn't even discuss it with family or friends for a while. I thought at the time that I was doing a pretty good job of hiding any problems I was having from them. Even today, some habits still remain in the way I relate to others. The way people view you can be so different to the way you really are. Many people have commented on how strong a person they think I am. I'm not really – I have insecurities like anyone else – I have just been pretty good at hiding them in the past and only showing the strong side.

I had a conversation with a friend of my husband's in September 2002, at a wedding in Cork. She could not understand, as she was very good friends with my husband, why we were not the best of friends also. That doesn't necessarily follow. People need a lot more in common to forge a friendship, such as shared interests, a common outlook on life and much more. I don't mean to generalise when I speak of adopted people, but those who I know tend to be the same. We offer as much information as we are comfortable with, depending on how well we know someone. But there is a fine line regarding how close we allow people to come. Some pieces of information we prefer to keep private and, speaking for myself, when dealing with someone who is very open and quite determined to bond with me and get me to open up, well, the opposite will happen. I tend to close up, offer the confident persona I want them to see and shut down all else.

Today I still let people in at my own pace and find it very hard when people try to force me to open up if I am not ready. Certainly this is not unusual in many human relationships, involving adopted people or not, but for me it concerned my own ability to allow people in to see the real me and that just takes time. I used to care what people thought of me; these days it doesn't bother me so much. I am what I am and, you know, I don't have to apologise for that to anyone. I do have certain personality quirks that stem from past experiences and, more to the point, from being adopted. But, like a fine wine, I am getting better with age - more full-bodied than I might have wished for, but that too can change!

Even now, I choose carefully the people I allow to get close to me, and even more carefully the people I show my insecurities and fears to. Watching a film recently, I wrote down the following phrase: 'Isn't it wonderful? We get to choose the people who we let into our weird little worlds.' It really is true. People are so quick to judge these days. If someone can't find an answer for something, they make up an answer. If you don't understand someone, why not simply ask them, 'What's up?'

There is one thing I have learned in the past few years. I may not be perfect at forging relationships, but if people don't care enough to get to know you then they're not worth it. Also you've got to take chances in life. You cannot wrap yourself up in cotton wool because you're afraid of what *might* happen. I hate to think what I would have missed out on if I had carried on wrapped up in my fears – in fact, ruled by them – as I was in earlier years.

I have learned it's important to take one step at a time. Everyone is different and there are some people you can trust and others you cannot, but not everyone is setting you up for a fall. I have realised that I cannot simply continue judging others using the excuse that because one woman gave me up for adoption people are not to be trusted. This sounds ridiculous when I read the words. You might feel the same. But as a child, when you live your life with this understanding, it becomes your safety net, the way you tend to judge others.

I am lucky, I love living and I love learning, much of which has come from the example of my family. So I suppose I will get better at forging relationships as time passes – I'm certainly having a lot of fun trying. I have met some of my best friends while enjoying a drink on holidays, and I cherish their friendship. I've learned that if you trust just a little and give people the benefit of the doubt just for a short while, you might be pleasantly surprised.

4

SAN ANTONIO

I love to love. I think I'm good at it. Family, both immediate and extended, are a vital part of my life. If I had to choose some of the most influential relationships in my life, those that have taught me so very much about life and myself, they would be those of my immediate family, Rachael and my mum's sister and her family. When considering writing about the subject of adoption, or indeed searching for my birth mother, I thought first and foremost of my family. Adoption is not simply about me, the person who was adopted. My decision to search for my birth mother affected my family and extended family, and eventually another family I was blessed to find in Wicklow. It affected us all. Now, though, I'd like to talk about my family in Cork, my mother, father and sister.

Eileen Cashin. She's the only woman who can decide to go on a diet and religiously stick to her regime – willpower of steel! Going on holiday two years ago, having smoked for nearly thirty years, she decided to give up smoking. Simple as that. She is still a non-smoker. Mum has depths that I don't think I might ever fathom. Her qualities are such that I can only attempt to emulate – kindness, humour at the most needed times, loyalty, open-heartedness, immense patience (did I mention patience?), a generosity and thoughtfulness that has earned her such very true friends. She is an amazing mother, friend and wife and, above all a woman who believes nothing is hopeless and everything has a solution. She can also cook the most fantastic meal from nothing. I remember years ago, every Thursday, I'd come home to chocolate caramel squares and, after I had had my ration after dinner, they would be hidden from little hands. God bless her, but she raised a very determined child and I found them each and every time! With all that she's involved in, still keeping an eye on us and Dad, now he's retired, I have no idea where she gets such a positive energy from. At thirty-two, I need her in my life more than ever and she always has something new to teach me.

My dad, Colum. My husband told me recently that I am most like Dad, personality wise, with bits of my mum thrown in for good measure. I can't think of a better mix, really. It's funny, people say that dogs grow to behave and look like their owners. As an adopted child, there are at least two occasions I can recall when friends stopped Dad on the street and told us that I was the image of him. Dad has the ability to make harmless jokes about others and himself, and I will always recall the phrase he used to use, laughing, with me in mind: 'You're like Murphy's old dog – you can give it, but you can't take it!' I'm still learning that lesson. Dad has a great sense of humour and is well able to hop the ball and tell a joke as quick as lightning. I have memories of water fights at 3 a.m. with his sister and brothers or dancing to Dean Martin or Frank Sinatra in the wee hours after a party. To choose only a few qualities I admire in Dad: he's a hard grafter and dedicated to any job he starts until it's completed perfectly, a loyal man and so very loving, always a family man, who still enjoys his children. At sixty-nine years of age he will run to the TV at the mention of *Tom and Jerry*. He has the capacity to understand and accept those he loves and envelop you in a safe place, no matter what you've done. He can make you feel special, as if you're the only one that counts, and he values his friends above all else. Both Mum and Dad are born entertainers and can hold a tune with the best of them.

Mum and Dad … they're exactly that. I smile to myself when people, especially those who know me well, ask me how my mother and father are. I reply, 'Oh, great, they're just back from holiday,' until I realise from the embarrassed silence facing me that they meant my birth mother and father. It's funny how people looking in on a situation perceive the lie of the land. Rachael and I feel the same, that no matter what went on before we arrived in Cork or that others may have loved us in some way before this, our parents are those who nurtured us and created a safe home for us. I don't mean to hurt those I have found or imply that a love does not exist for my new birth family, because it does, but this is simply what our hearts tell us. Mum and Dad make me laugh, they still dry my tears when I can't learn a violin piece, they know me better than I know myself at times and I love them with a passion that knows no boundaries. Over the years, since the first time as a young child when I questioned their love for me, they have shown me I can trust them with anything. Mum always taught me, as her mother did her, no matter what happens in my life, to bring a problem home if I need to and we will face it together.

I found myself a part of this family after they had experienced the great loss of their second daughter. They waited and made the decision to adopt only after much consideration and thought and guidance from God, I believe. I know they don't regret their decision to adopt, but it has been hard at times for them. It *is* different adopting a child. They did not love me any less, but it has brought its own challenges, for them all. Mum has told me stories about the six months before my adoption was made legal that astound me. Imagine having a child for six months, and loving that baby for every minute of that time, before the adoption is made legal, before they knew without a doubt that I would not be taken away from them.

The district nurse arrived at our home one day during the six months to check how Mum was getting on and I had a terrible nappy rash. Mum tells me she was so worried the nurse would think she was incapable of looking after me properly. I really can't imagine what that must be like. As Mum says herself, they didn't have to do that for Mary. But adopted I was and I changed their lives – for the better, I hope. For better or worse …

There are some things that I would like to change about the system if I were ever to adopt a child, but I think perhaps that I am not selfless enough to provide such a close-to-perfect family home for a child who is adopted. I have no idea how my family managed to shower me with such love and provide such a secure safety blanket, which I clung to for many years. The words 'safety blanket' in earlier years meant for me the knowledge that my family's love would never be withdrawn, that I could trust them and they would never intentionally hurt me. Eileen and Colum Cashin's patience and love still astounds me today. Thus this has been one of the most difficult chapters to write. Adoption brings with it issues and challenges that deserve further examination, not just for my family's benefit, but for others who will also try to do a wonderful job, like my family did with me. The only thing I can say to those people is good luck.

From what the years of healing have taught me, I hope I can offer some advice. The words, thoughts and feelings I have to offer on the subject come from the heart and have no malice in them. They merely carry the hope that they might offer some guidance to those who either have already adopted a child or are considering it for the future. There are no hard and fast rules, only my experiences, for what they are worth.

This chapter was born from a question my father asked me on the way back from Dublin in July 2003, before I had begun to write an account of my experience of adoption. I choose the word 'born' as it indicates a new stage in our lives, how on this day on the way back from Dublin my relationship with my parents changed in some way. Due to my father's honesty, I have grown much more accepting of my need to have my birth family in my life and I know now that Mum and Dad are 100 per cent supportive of this need. Our relationship has become more open in many ways, and I am learning to acknowledge my own needs and at times put them first.

My birth brother from Wicklow had been in a bad motorbike accident and was in intensive care in Dublin and both Mum and Dad had accompanied me on the train to see them all. On the way back on the train, Dad asked me the most astounding question either of them had ever asked me. For the first time, he asked me: 'Would you change the fact that you were adopted if you could?' I can tell you now I was speechless. So many thoughts crossed my mind. Thoughts of how just a little bit of my parents' insecurity still remained following my search, thoughts of my sister, thoughts of how much I loved them in Cork, thoughts of how I wouldn't intentionally hurt one hair on any of their heads.

The truth of the matter is that, at that time, I simply did not have the answer. I had not assimilated my own thoughts and was not able to quieten my soul regarding what I had done, what I had learned about the past or myself and what the future held. I simply told him he was being an eejit, that I adored them and was the luckiest girl in the world. I loved my mum, dad and sister more than anything in the world. But my mum and dad had asked me the most honest question of my life, and it must have taken a lot of courage to do that. I believe they were prepared for the answer one way or the other. I owe them an attempt to answer that question truthfully. Here it is. Mary, for all the things I have not said, this is for you, because I love you.

It has taken many years for the thoughts in this chapter to become clear. The relationship between my sister and me has been hard for my parents at times. I remember one Christmas night a war of bitter words broke out at home between Mary and myself. Mum and Aunty Mary from England were witness to it. We screamed harsh words at each other without regard for others in the family, as was, in hindsight, quite normal I suppose, between siblings with such a large age gap. Mum ended up in tears in the kitchen because she could not understand the venom and strong feelings between Mary and me. We retired to our own rooms while Mum cried at the kitchen table, desperately trying to figure out how to fix what she perceived as a problem. Mum loves to fix things and she's good at it. She has a talent for soothing waters and one of her favourite sayings is 'When thunder roars you've just got to listen to it.' Here was one problem, though, that was causing her heartache and neither Mary nor I seemed to care.

Now I can't even remember what the quarrel was about. Probably about some piece of clothing I took without Mary's permission! That night, Aunty Mary came into each of our rooms, dried our tears and calmed the waters for a short while. This was to be the pattern for a number of years. Siblings fight. It's normal. We love each other very much. I do believe, however, that there were underlying issues that needed to be sorted. A saying comes to mind when I think of my sister Mary – still waters run deep.

When trying to understand the dynamic between Mary and I, recently I've smiled and thought of the very basic relationship between dogs in a family home. Aidan and I love dogs and have done some research into what experts call the 'top dog', because of what was going on at home with our own dogs. This 'top dog' usually tends to be the leader and one who takes no prisoners. I have had experience of one dog in particular who, although he was the first to become the family pet and by virtue of this would have been expected to rule the roost, was only interested in where the next meal was coming from, when the ball would be thrown and how best to secure attention and love. This in itself was not the problem.

When another dog was introduced to the scenario, matters escalated quickly. This second dog was a rescue dog, a mongrel not wanted by her owners. She was terribly nervous for most of her life, unsure of her position and in need of a huge amount of time, reassurance and loving. In fact, she craved this love and attention. Here were two dogs, both in need of love and care, yet one was by far the stronger personality and won the attention more often than not.

Mary, I love her to death. She's caring, considerate and God help anyone who would hurt me. I feel the same way about her. There have been times in my early twenties when I feared for the lives of those who hurt me – she hated them enough for both of us! When I lost a job, she was there to ridicule it with me, simply to make me feel better. If I worried about something, she would make me laugh. If I shed tears, she would be there to wipe them – she still is.

I had a conversation with a friend recently. I had called for a chat and we were discussing my search for my birth mother, the new family, how we got on and what I've learned. She was listening to my thoughts and feelings and the difficulties I was having and helping me. Our chat turned to past years, when Mary and I were growing up. What I'm about to write may be uncomfortable reading for Mum and Dad, and for Mary, but everything was said with love and deep regard for you all. Even now I can feel tears welling up because I love Mary and hate the thought that I might not have been the only one to have been hurt over the years.

This friend laughed and told me that, as a child, I was spoiled and Mary, possibly, was of the age to notice everything. Perhaps there are those in my family who saw things that as a child I was oblivious to. Mary was on her own for ten years and then I came along. It's not simply a matter of one child's jealousy towards another because they have stolen the limelight, because I don't think it was jealousy that Mary felt as a child. Perhaps it was a confusion and an inability at such a young age to understand this needy child who had found her way into their midst.

Dad told me a few years ago that, as Mary was their first born, they were quite nervous with her and wanted to do everything right. They were also very young when she arrived. They muddled through and learned a lot. I arrived and they had the previous years' experience under their belt and, as many have said, I was a bit of a mad child and made people laugh. They simply had the confidence, nothing more, to perhaps enjoy me and relax a bit more. They did not love me any more than Mary – they never have and never will. We are loved equally and we have always been given every opportunity. We each made our own choices. For others outside the home, it might be easy to simply say I was spoiled, and they are indeed right, but there was so much more.

I was a child that needed constant affection and reassurance, and when I was given that love and affection, I would look for more, just to make sure. I don't know how Mum and Dad did it, but they dedicated themselves to making sure I knew, and had no doubt in my mind, that I was loved above all else and that I was needed and wanted. I must have hung out of them and taken every ounce of their energy. As I get a little older, I wonder how much of their time and love I 'stole' from Mary – not intentionally but because it was just what my heart needed. I have wondered at the ability and maturity of a little girl, Mary, to be able to understand what was happening. Can a child understand that her sister simply needed a lot of love and reassurance, not that Mum and Dad loved her any more? Did Mary understand that, as their child who was born to them, she really had nothing to worry about, that their love was guaranteed? Maybe in my own way, although no memory of this comes to mind, I was threatened by the knowledge that Mary actually grew in our mummy's tummy and I didn't. All I know for certain is that we were two little girls who both needed love, and I think the stronger personality might have pushed her way in a little bit more. It was not a conscious move. I was just a little girl who needed a lot of love and, for all her funny and mad ways, just a little girl who was very unsure of herself.

Only recently, my Uncle Pa described me as a very confident and outgoing person. I suppose I am in some ways now, having learned a lot about myself in the last number of years. I was not always so self-assured, however. As childhood gave way to adolescence, and a few turbulent and angry years and the realisation of what being adopted actually meant in adult terms, I think the differences between Mary and I grew for a while. I simply needed to find a cure for what ailed me.

A few years ago I started a search that was to answer many questions for me and provide me with a confidence and sense of respect and esteem for myself that had been lacking for some time. I found my roots. I rid myself of some ghosts. But what worries me is that I believe Mary still has some insecurities and is, as yet, unable to talk to me about them. Mary still feels threatened by this new birth family, whether because we have the same DNA or because we get on very well, I am not sure, but a part of it still remains.

On my birthday in March 2005, Mary and I were sitting at the kitchen table and we began to chat about the house she was building in Kerry. I had spent a while in hospital before Christmas 2004 and was still recovering so I was unable to travel. A few weeks earlier Mary had asked me to visit Kerry to see their house, which was at foundation level at that stage, but, I couldn't manage the journey, so I said I was not yet able to see it but would see it as soon as I could. A month after this I was on the slow road back to full health and Aidan said he would bring me to see the gang in Wicklow, as I had not seen them since early November and had missed out on seeing them at Christmas. But this afternoon in March, Mary mentioned my visit to the family in Wicklow and was quite upset that I could visit them but yet not take a trip down to see her new site in Kerry. I tried to explain that I had begun to feel a bit better and I had not seen them in months but that I would see her site soon, and I was very much looking forward to seeing it.

I also tried to explain to Mary again that, even though these birth brothers and sisters had entered my life and were becoming special to me, they could never replace the love I feel for her. She did not seem convinced. I tried again. I talked to her about the last thirty-one years and all the times she cleaned my grazed knees or dried my tears when I broke up with a boyfriend or had a fight with a friend and so many other times when we conspired together as sisters. I told her that those years of two people growing up together, looking out for one another and caring for each other can never be replaced by anyone. The Wicklow gang can never be a part of those years, as they are sacred memories between Mary and I. The relationships I build with them are of a different sort and, while I grow to love them, I have enough love in my heart for everyone.

Maybe I contributed to her insecurities because I decided to search for my birth family ten years ago, and if so, I apologise, but it was not by design. We are both loved equally by our parents and we love each other. We do now and we always will. Nothing will change that.

As a child, Mary did not want me to know that I was different to her in any way. At only ten or eleven Mary looked up to Mum and asked her, 'Do we really have to tell Claire she's adopted?' What special words from just a little girl. They give an insight into the person that she was and still is today. This is a poem that Mary wrote for me, when I was just a baby:

My baby sister, I love her, I love her,
but sometimes she's bold.
Her name is Claire and she's six months old.
She is very funny and she's her mother's pet.
Don't put anything in front of her,
Unless you want it torn and wet.
She is a little doll and as cute as can be.
She's the best baby in the world,
And I hope you agree.

I don't understand why I was never too threatened by the fact that Mary was 'theirs' 100 per cent. Maybe a small part of me kept that fact at the back of my mind, but I think it has to do with Mary's approach to me. I was her sister and in her mind that was all there was to it.

So, to answer the question, would I change being adopted? Let me put it this way: if I could turn back the clock and take away some of Mary's hurt because of adoption, I would give my right arm to do so. My behaviour in later teenage years was unacceptable and, although it was merely hurt and confusion finding their way to the surface, more often than not it was Mary who felt the full force of my anger. If I could take away the hurt and pain I experienced and, more importantly, the hurt I have caused those who loved me, yes, I would change *some* of that in a heartbeat. If I changed all of it then I might be a different person.

But would I change being a Cashin and being adopted? Not if you offered me all the money in the world. A year or two ago the answer might have been a little different, but that's only because of the pain and grief of loss, feelings of what might have been. When I visit Wicklow now and my birth family there, I still experience some of the loss of not knowing a large immediate family. When you are a part of the ball hopping and love of a large group of people, then it's natural to think of how things could have been different.

That does not affect the love I feel for my mum, dad and sister. They are my family, and they have been my life for so long and will continue to be for as long as God sees fit. Getting to know the gang in Wicklow is also very special and I feel blessed they came into my life. They have given me an amazing gift – the gift of acceptance. I don't know what the master plan is but, hopefully, one day I'll find out and things will sit perfectly in my mind, heart and soul. Everything will fall into place.

5
WHAT'S DEEP INSIDE

There have been times when turmoil and confusion were part of my life, but they came in waves as I matured. There is nothing unique about this, as most people have to overcome troubles in their lives. I simply reached the other side. When trying to describe what I felt throughout the years, I am worried that it will read like some terrible saga, without hope, without an end. But it is a happy story. Any instance when we are lucky enough to rediscover ourselves and manage to become whole is an amazing gift. But as with all of the most valuable lessons in life, sometimes it's not as easy as we might wish. But how can we enjoy the silver lining without first having to dry off after the downpour?

I hate to be defined merely as an adopted person, hurt, scared, consisting of no other depth to my personality. There is more to Claire Cashin, such as my impish sense of humour (as my father-in-law described it once), my passion for music, for animals and for life itself. So this chapter, though serious and intended to offer some insight into the reality of adoption, is not meant to suggest that my life as an adopted person will be forever scarred. It's just a process we have to reason out, in our own time, like any challenge or loss that is faced in life. Nothing is insurmountable.

I hope that I can, in some way, explain in simple words what adoption *can be* for many adopted people. Understanding the psyche of an adopted person is half the battle. So these words are for anyone who might love an adopted person and wish to support them, whatever their choices in life might be. My parents have always managed to grasp that, even though they did everything in their power to protect me from pain in my life, this was one journey I had to go on myself. We were all well aware that, even though it would bring pain and revelations, it would be a worthwhile journey.

Many have written about the possible effect on a newborn baby after separation from its mother and an immediate parting from her. Do babies already bond with the mother in the womb, and if this woman is immediately missing from our lives, does this create a gaping void? I don't know the answer or how a theory like this can be proved. From my own experience, having waited for six weeks before joining my family in Cork, I find it hard to understand why any child can't be given to its new family as soon as possible. Why not promote early bonding with the new family and in this way ensure the child is blessed with an abundance of soft touches, loving lullabies and genuine devotion from another human being as early as possible?

Some of the teachings in the study of adoption still have to be tested and proven as fact. Adoption itself, however, and its effect on any child is *not* a theory. Most of what I write about in this chapter has its groundings in fact. I know because I have lived much of my life in this fashion, only to realise I had to change many of my beliefs as I searched, with the help of those close to me. It's never easy letting go of hard-held beliefs, lifelines that you hold firm to in order to protect yourself. Such is life. It's certainly one hell of a learning process.

It's very important, especially in the context of family life, that open communication between children and adoptive parents about all aspects of adoption be maintained. Nothing should be taboo, as this will help children to adjust. The children cannot avoid many of the questions they will be faced with as they mature – questions like, who was my mum? Why did she have me adopted? Did she not love me? Being able to talk honestly about feelings and hurts will help when they need to examine their beliefs and voice their insecurities.

I have wondered how hard it might be for many birth mothers to accept that no matter how much they wanted to keep their babies, and no matter what selfless reasons they had for relinquishing him or her, the child may still experience a trauma of separation and, in turn, abandonment. I am conscious of Mai and Tony, my birth parents, reading my words and finding them hard to understand and being hurt by them. I hope they know me well enough by now to know that I do not feel any anger or malice towards them because of their decision to have me adopted. Why would I when their decision has guaranteed such love and devotion in my life! My words are not meant to hurt them, but if I hope to offer any help to parents who intend to adopt or already are facing behavioural issues with their adoptive children, then it would be no good to skirt around the very real and raw emotional issues of adoption. It would serve no purpose at all.

I always understood that my birth mother had relinquished all rights to me because she wanted to give me the best in life, something she herself could not offer. I *understood* why she had to give me up, but it never made me *feel* any better. I didn't care why she did it. It was still 'done to me' and I still felt abandoned. At times growing up, people said to me, 'You should know that she did what was best for you – she did what she did out of love for you.' I suppose I believed if she loved me so much, then how could she bear to part with me. Who knows? One thing I do know to be true, however, is that I have always had an ache in my heart and a sense of loss. Something was missing.

The day I was married, Dad told a story about when I was six or maybe seven years of age. Mum would get up every morning at about 7.30 to help me get ready for school. But I was having none of it – I would arrange my own uniform and dress myself, thank you very much! If Mum was up at 7.30 then I would set my alarm for 7.15 the next day. The next morning Mum would rise at 7.15 and I would rise at 7.00 the day after. Dad made it sound as if it was mere wilfulness and determination to be independent but perhaps it was something deeper.

I remember also tearing my dress at about age six, and as Mum began to mend the sleeve, I grabbed the garment, determined to sew it together myself. Needless to say, at such a young age my sewing skills were limited, but I was determined to do things for myself, not to be a burden. Can a child understand at six what it is to feel like a burden? Most definitely. I was so sensitive to the possibility that my parents' love might change that I was determined to be a good girl. I was aware even then of the chance they had given me, aware that they had 'chosen' me, and so I tried to do everything in my power to make them glad they had made this choice.

This determination to be self-sufficient was matched with a conscious decision on my part to be what I perceived others wanted, something that is quite common with adopted people. Often adopted children and adults try to become people pleasers, constantly seeking approval, determined to make their family proud – determined to avoid rejection. I have been guilty of this as a young adult. And this tendency to constantly try to be something else, in effect not myself, created problems in later years when trying to bond with people my own age. I have had to learn to allow myself to reveal any negative feelings and discover how to express myself openly and honestly. I suppose this was my defensive coping mechanism. If you don't admit to any 'bad' feelings, they don't exist, do they? I know I understood myself to be lacking in something, not quite good enough to be kept, and so, as something defective, I was adopted, second best.

I was always very insecure and at the same time terrified of people seeing this insecurity. If I kept the mask on, I was more in control. Many adopted people, like myself, do not even realise they are wearing this mask. It's a discipline that comes naturally to them. As I grew older, however, this way of acting became exhausting and inside I became an angry person. The loss I was feeling was very real to me, and as I grew up, the need for mourning became acute, despite my best efforts to deny such feelings. The most frequently used defence against painful feelings and method of self-protection can be easily observed in an adopted person's denial and avoidance of these feelings. It can be very difficult to let down these defences because for the most part we are completely unaware that we are employing them.

I have often wondered about my relationship with my mum. Mum was always the person that I most needed to connect with, yet subconsciously I think I saw her as the most dangerous. From past experience I had learned that the mother cannot be trusted – she may be an 'adandoner'. Of course I loved Mum, but I can't help wondering if deep inside me there were feelings of betrayal, anger and sadness that I tried to project onto her.

Mum tells the story of how one Christmas, when I was a young teenager, I was brought into town to get a Christmas outfit. I was probably already a size eighteen! We traipsed all over town, into every shop, to try and find something that would fit. I tried on miniskirts, belly tops – everything that was all the rage at the time. Mum tried her hardest and, blessed with an abundance of patience, she kept a tight lip and tried to advise me as best and as delicately as she could. Eventually we found a pair of black flared trousers, a top and a 'posh' scarf to finish the outfit, the bill for which was well over and above Mum's budget. But we were both glad the ordeal was over and we could go home with an outfit. Walking down the main street in Cork, I lashed out at Mum, digging her in the arm, shouting at her in my most venomous tone, 'It's all your bloody fault anyway – you feed me too much!' My poor mother.

I don't know where this came from. Perhaps I wanted to hurt her for some reason that I could not yet understand. I was always loved, always told I was so very 'special', but to be chosen or special can be such a burden to bear. To retain this status of being special, to retain the love and acceptance of my parents, did I have to become perfect? I was *never once* aware of any pressure on me to live up to some expectation, but perhaps my own deep-seated convictions made me believe that I had to try and make the grade and be thankful to Mum and Dad for what they had given me, what they had 'rescued' me from. It's definitely something I have always believed, for if I heard these words once, I heard them a hundred thousand times from the lips of Mum and Dad: 'You don't owe us anything. Stop spending your money on us – we're the ones that feel grateful for what you've given us.' I heard the words but I did not listen to the message.

The need to prove how worthy we are of home and family, and the gratitude felt by many adoptees, results in many accomplished individuals among the adopted population. I do not by any means consider myself accomplished, but I did attend two colleges and succeeded (God only knows how!) in gaining two honours degrees for myself. Was it for me or was it so I could see the proud faces of my parents and know that I was a good child, worthy of their love? People say that adopted children are ever watchful of the environment, aware of shifts in their 'climate' so that they can adapt and provide the necessary behaviour or action. I have often been guilty of this over-sensitivity and the slightest whiff of disapproval would send me into fits of tears and worry. This exaggerated drama-queen behaviour tried my parents' patience day after day and I am lucky their love won out.

These issues of trust, love and permanency of relationships became an inescapable part of my personality as I became a young adult. I learned pretty quickly that if I did not put myself in a position to be hurt, if I avoided close relationships and distanced myself from others, I could defend against rejection. I was always the joker and had many friends, but not too many I was myself with. Who spends most of their life laughing?

One day in secondary school, in third year, I remember my teacher arriving into class with a face that would turn milk sour. She started a tirade, telling the class in a violent voice about one young girl who had the audacity to write on the test last week that she had not managed to do any study for the test and had handed up her paper with this explanation. Ten points for guessing who the young girl was.

My classmates and I still laugh at this story. It *is* a funny moment, yet at the time I will never forget the damage it did. My gran was very sick, and maybe it was the beginning of difficult emotions regarding loss pushing through, but when I was challenged in front of the class – 'Would Ms Cashin like to give us all an explanation as to why she thought it appropriate to write this on her paper?' – I stood up and started to cry so hard. In front of thirty teenagers, I cried and said, 'I didn't do any study because I didn't have the time and my granny has Alzheimer's!' I know, I know. It's funny. But at the time I had no idea where these emotions had burst forth from and I felt such shame and ridicule that day with the class laughing. If I was delicate and wary before this, afterwards I was downright vulnerable.

At about this time, aged fifteen, something in me darkened. There was a distinct shift in my emotions. I knew instinctively these new feelings were dangerous and must be kept hidden at all costs. It wasn't easy, though, as I found myself becoming very angry. I raised hell at home with tantrums, picking fights with Mary, and got into trouble at school. Oppositional behaviour and an intense rage towards my parents were practically a daily event, probably due to the subconscious depth of my feelings, which were denied in order to protect myself. As thoughts of my birth mother began to creep in, I slowly began to feel the start of pain, the fear of loss, the belief that she did not love me enough to keep me, and if I gave in to these feelings, these emotions would worsen and become more intense. It was far safer for me to try and shut them out, to deny them.

My fear of rejection, too, affected all my relationships deeply as I grew older. I have now managed to let go of much of it, but one aspect of my personality repeats itself constantly, and it's something Aidan, my husband, finds hard to understand. People get only one chance with me. I will try to get to know anyone, but if they hurt me, that's it. It's time to say goodbye. I shut the door on that person and I don't let them back in. You leave my life, then that's it, forever! It's a bad trait to have. Forgiveness is precious and I'm learning, but this has hurt many people who have known me in past years.

All these issues, and more, impinged upon my development as a young individual. I choose the word individual because I realise that adoption affects everyone in a different way. Many issues stayed with me up until very recently and have affected some of the most rewarding relationships in my life.

6

LOVE IS ...

I grew up with a preconceived idea of what love should be and what it can be. In earlier years I was insecure about many things, but the one place I was sure I was *always* loved was between the four walls of my home – my haven and my refuge when times got bad. I still lean on my family too much, I know, but it took many years for me to accept once and for all that I was loved and accepted *for me*, plain and simple. I pushed the boundaries again and again to see if they would still be there for me. I even believed that I might have been second best, their second choice.

At about age fourteen, I had a really bad fight with my family one Sunday afternoon. Confusion, hurt, anger and questions concerning my birth mother had begun to creep in, and rather than reveal this pain to my parents I tried to hide it, but it was becoming difficult to keep it from them. This particular Sunday I went out of my way to be difficult, to avoid doing the dishes after lunch, and I picked a fight with everyone at home. I cried wildly and screamed accusations at them that they really didn't love me. I remember hearing the words, 'Oh great, here we go again. Could you just stop this drama-queen behaviour?' Instead of realising that I should sit down with them and talk about my feelings, all I took from these words was confirmation of what I had always feared: they did not understand me and their love was conditional on my being a good daughter.

I was finding it more difficult to deliver this good behaviour as the months passed. So I ran out of the house and down towards the river Lee, just because it was a place where I would sit quietly by myself to think and watch the ducks float by. Dad followed me without my knowledge and spotted me standing at the edge of the water looking in. By the time I spotted him and before he had a chance to catch up with me, I ran quickly up an embankment without being seen. When he reached the spot where I had been standing, well, for a short time, he actually considered the worst. Perhaps I realised what he must have been thinking at that moment, and for a few seconds I hesitated to come out from hiding to make him sorry for not understanding my pain, for not accepting it as a part of me and loving me still. But I had calmed down and a hug awaited me. Recently he talked of this day to me and about the real fear he had felt, but I was just trying to test them and see how far I could push them before my behaviour became 'unlovable'. Their love never stopped.

There are times I wonder how I had the audacity to do some of the things I did. We visited close friends of Mum and Dad's when I was six. I went upstairs to the bathroom while Mum and Dad were downstairs, and on returning to the room I spotted a £5 note. I was brazen enough to slip the money inside my pocket. We arrived home later that day and the phone rang. It was Mum's friend, who made no big deal of it, yet for my sake thought it best to confess to Mum. I still cringe at the memory! I was brought back to the house and made to knock on the door and give back the money and say how sorry I was. For that, and worse, Mum and Dad, I am so very sorry!

I have learned that love is not measured against anything. It's not conditional. It's not dependent on how well you do or how many friends you have. It took many years for me to finally accept that I could show them the worst of me and still nothing would change. What I have since come to realise is that my behaviour was something that they might not have liked or accepted, but that loving me and liking me as a person were two entirely different things. As I grew older, however, I learned that the love of your family was very different to the love between a man and a woman.

Since the age of approximately seventeen, I have never been a single person. I have always had a boyfriend. I don't know if that stems from a need to have someone next to me constantly or the belief that if I was part of a couple, I was worthy of love. I hate to have to admit to either scenario. It's not even that I was terribly good at being someone's girlfriend, but simply that I liked it. It was easier to be someone's other half than on my own, unsure of what I wanted from life. I was never very good at knowing what I wanted, but I was *very* good at figuring out what others wanted and playing my part in giving that to them.

Don't get me wrong – I wasn't a complete idiot. You could push me so far and I'd go beserk, but more often than not I was willing to accept anything for a quiet life. If I could turn back the clock, I would do things differently. There are many men I wouldn't look twice at and a few 'friends' I would have lost a lot earlier. When I consider how I allowed some boyfriends to treat me in the past, well, I am not proud of it. One in particular, whom I had been seeing for close to a year, had been invited to a cousin's wedding, and it would have been the first time he would meet most of my family. He promised to be there and I waited and waited, and even at midnight I still believed there must be a reasonable explanation, that he would still arrive. He never did, and the following day I merely accepted his excuse and kissed him and hid the fact that I was terribly disappointed in him and so very hurt.

After this night, and many more like them, I had more or less given him permission to treat me in this way and had really only myself to blame.

Today I know loyalty, fidelity, trust, respect, honesty and compassion to be some of the most important qualities between two people, but when younger I accepted much less, due to either lack of self-respect or a need in me to feel wanted, at any cost. The best lessons are the ones you learn the hard way. Maybe I wouldn't change too much. If I did, I may not have met the one man in my life who has helped me become the person I am today, my best friend, Aidan.

I met Aidan initially through one of his friends, whom I began dating at the age of about nineteen – just one of those relationships that teaches you lessons about many things. My relationship with Aidan was the first in which I truly felt that this was a man I could possibly trust, in time. I realised quite early on that I did not have to spend every minute of our time together with only his happiness in mind. I really do believe that I was meant to meet Aidan, but when we first met I was actually quite afraid of Aidan Murphy! We were on the beach in Ardmore one weekend, water skiing, and the craic was good. Alan, a good friend, had invented a new method of water skiing using his rear end as skis. When the fun finished and the boat had to be brought back to the campsite, I was asked to accompany Aidan in the car. I will never forget the way I felt that day – 'Oh my God! What am I going to say to this man?' I was really nervous, despite all the smiles and effort made by Aidan. We both laugh when we think back to that first meeting. But it wasn't long before we realised we had a few things in common.

Things with Aidan's friend didn't last long, a year, but long enough to make me realise what a silly girl I had been. Aidan was engaged to someone at that time, and it became obvious to us that we were both in relationships that made us unhappy, spending most of the time fighting with our partners over one thing or another. As a result, we became firm friends. I was attending Shannon College of Hotel Management at this time, and it wasn't long before I was off to London as part of my course. Aidan and I had been good friends for the best part of a year at this stage and we kept in contact while I was away.

Mutual friends began to imply we were interested in each other and would suggest that we looked lovely together. Sometimes during a telephone conversation with me a friend would say that Aidan had mentioned missing me, or vice versa. So I believed that Aidan had taken a fancy to me and the feeling was mutual. Using the foundation we had already built, and after each of us had broken up with our respective partners, we had our first kiss one weekend when I was home from London. When I returned to London, we began a long-distance relationship. Aidan's patience and genuine care during these years was certainly a very important influence in my life at that time.

I worked in London for nearly two years, until I eventually finished college, and Aidan and myself spent a fortune, not only on flights to and from London, but also on phone calls practically every night. It was a time of many happy memories, far too many to count. My mum's brother and his family were also based in London and looked after me well, always keeping a watchful eye on me. Each and every one of the family was looking out for me and today we're closer than ever. It's because of those early years in London that I am lucky enough to have made such very true friends.

Another year passed and eventually I had had enough and I made the decision to come home. Aidan came over for me, and I have no idea how we made it home with everything in the back of his poor Lancia, but make it home we did. Those early years are some of the most important of our relationship. Like any couple, we've had our ups and downs along the way, but, well, what doesn't kill you makes you stronger! I was happy to finally be home, where I felt safe once more, and was lucky enough to have a home where I was welcomed into the fold again.

On the surface things seemed fine to everyone – everyone but Aidan, that is. We settled into a routine. I was working in hotels at this time as restaurant manager and duty manager, and I spent time with Aidan whenever I was off duty. I was not terribly happy in the industry and it put quite a strain on us both. We grabbed time whenever we could. I have wondered since why my emotions concerning adoption got the better of me around this time and the only answer I can come up with is that it was because I began to depend on Aidan and needed to know once and for all if he really and truly loved me. Sure, we had discussed getting married and we had made plans, but he had yet to see the real me, the frightened girl who questioned her worth and was ashamed of being adopted, ashamed of not being worthy of love. I was unsure how he would react to the real me and I certainly didn't yet trust him. I was faced with the realisation that unless Aidan knew me, and everything about me, we wouldn't be able to make a go of things at all.

That said, I didn't even know myself that well yet. After all, it was Aidan who eventually figured out what was missing and what I needed to do. The sequence of events for the next two years of our relationship is hard to unravel and I can only try to explain, as best I can, what I believe I was trying to do.

I already cared deeply for Aidan and needed him, but I was so unsure of his feelings towards me and was so afraid of being hurt and rejected, that I did the only thing I knew how to do back then: I tested his feelings for me, again and again, as I used to do with my family at home. Not the ideal solution under the circumstances, simply because neither myself nor Aidan understood what was happening. I didn't have the maturity or the ability to communicate my fears and feelings, because to do so would have left me open to being hurt and abandoned, as I saw it. The only man I had utterly trusted until this moment in my life had been my father, and I was not willing to let go of that safety net without a fight. At this stage, Aidan and I had been together for over two years.

I turned my frustration and anger, which were bubbling very close to the surface, towards the one person who I was terrified of being hurt by – Aidan. We would attend a party or function, which would start out as great fun. The night would progress and I would drink quite a lot, so that by the end of the night I was incapable of dealing with any emotions. I think many family and extended family members believed my fits of rage and 'attention seeking' were merely due to immaturity. I *was* immature, in the sense that I had no clue how to deal with some very raw issues of self-esteem, trust, intimacy with another human being and honesty with others and with myself. But the fits of rage that Aidan witnessed were more to do with an inability to admit I had some very real problems with being adopted. I drank far too much at the weekends in those early years, from my late teens into my early twenties, using drink as a crutch of sorts.

When I was drunk, I could let loose my emotions, and it was such a relief not to have to hide them any more, despite how difficult everyone around me found them. Aidan did not know how to react to my anger. After a skinful of booze, if I caught him catching someone's eye, I screamed at him that he didn't love me. After a rage of this kind, if he returned to the party, I screamed at him that he didn't care enough about me to stay and comfort me. (Who would, really, when all they would get was abuse?) This was the way most of our nights out ended for many months.

The day after a night like this, when sober, I refused to talk about the night before and tried to make up for my behaviour by cooking a nice dinner, for example. I was unable to admit that I needed to start being honest with myself about my feelings about being an adopted person. I thought I could control my emotions very well, without drink at least, and so could keep any feelings of confusion and hurt at bay. It was this build-up of emotions that began to eat away at me, and as time passed I needed the release of anger so I drank more and more and used those nights as a pressure valve to let off steam. When I had drink taken it became evident to Aidan that I trusted him enough to show him, the only way I knew how, that I was having problems and, even though I was unable to talk openly about what was inside, that my behaviour was a cry for help and I couldn't find the answers alone.

I have screamed at him and accused him of not loving me when the only thing I really needed was a hug and some reassurance. I have often hurt him more with my tongue than I ever could have physically. It got to the stage for Aidan when he knew the end of the night would bring a 'fit' of some sort and the tears would come either silently or accompanied by abuse of some sort towards him. But he began to show me that I should be proud of myself and I began to slowly trust him.

My behaviour during that time was unacceptable, and even though it was a real cry for help and not selfishness or a wish to treat others badly, it is still not reason enough to scream abuse at people who try to help you. I have privately expressed my gratitude, thanks and love to Aidan for those years and for helping me to admit to things I was terrified of facing.

People sometimes do not realise that when an adopted person has been hurt it can take a long, long time to recover from this hurt, something that another person might bounce back from quickly. A hurtful act can throw me back to earlier years and feelings of deep insecurity. People might think I am very strong, and I *can* be, but regarding my feelings and how I can hurt, I'm the sensitive type – too sensitive. I am what I am, however, and while there are some things about me that might need a bit of fine tuning, I am always trying to be a better person, more caring, more considerate, less defensive, and I firmly believe that, no matter what age, we *can* change and become better people.

There are still times, rare though they are, when I find myself reverting to old behaviours, when I find it hard to forgive, for example. Everyone hurts sometimes, and we always hurt those we love the most, and I find my insecurities can creep back in. But I listen to Aidan now and I know how to see sense and reason with myself. I know now things will be all right. The sense of despair has left me. It might be easier to understand how this evolved when I tell you the story of what spurred me into action and what forced my hand – something that made me really and truly look at myself in the mirror.

This particular night could have been the end of Aidan and myself. Aidan was very quiet all night and he dropped me home in the wee hours of the morning. He sat there looking troubled, staring out the window. He tried to tell me how he could not see himself marrying someone like me, because of the way I had been carrying on over the past year. He had simply had enough and, although he did love me, he could only accept so much. He told me that he believed the way I was acting was not part of the real Claire and he thought he knew the reason for it. When prompted, he said he felt I really needed to admit a few things, namely that I needed to search for my birth mother and find answers to some questions that were haunting me.

I was horrified at his honesty and, while I realised deep down the truth of his words, I was terrified of admitting that I was so unhappy. I got out of the car, slammed the door and decided that was that. We were finished. I cried a lot and lay awake most of that night. With hindsight, perhaps all I had heard from Aidan that night was, 'I don't love you enough to help you. I can't be bothered to try and understand what it is you need from me.' Worst of all,

I think, was my inability to understand my own feelings. In my mind, it was safer to just walk away from Aidan.

We did not speak for nearly four weeks but the words Aidan had said made me look at myself honestly for the first time in my life. I thought long and hard about everything that Aidan had said to me and that he did probably love me, and that each word he had spoken he had said with my best interests at heart. I realised that he knew the best and worst of me and simply wanted to help me. I also knew that I had tried to keep my feelings of confusion and pain locked up inside me and now I was exhausted and things had to change – Aidan was right. As I accepted everything Aidan said as truth, I was forced to try to understand why I would want to look for someone who had given me away, when I had been so happy with my family, blessed with love and every opportunity in life. I loved them as if I had grown in Eileen Cashin's womb. What was wrong with me? Why was this upsetting me so much? Coupled with the realisation that I had much to change in my life was my fear of trusting this man and letting him get so close to me.

To need Aidan yet to be afraid of admitting I needed him so much, and therefore admitting my vulnerability, was terrifying. *I* didn't need anyone in my life. I wasn't going to let anyone, certainly not Aidan, get close enough to hurt me, to reject me and crush me. It was a matter of protecting myself and hurting Aidan before he hurt me, which in my eyes was inevitable, not knowing how to trust anyone outside of the family unit. Past relationships had also taught me this. There was neither sense nor reason to the way I had things sorted in my mind. I had no knowledge or experience of what a relationship between a man and woman should be. I'm still learning … however slowly!

I have had many conversations with people over the past years and one in particular touched my heart. I was told a story last year over dinner in a restaurant. A friend of mine revealed that her husband had given up a little boy for adoption many years before they married. Now this boy, Adam, had contacted her husband and both families, the adoptive family and the boy's birth father, had begun communicating. Just before Christmas, the boy's adoptive mother had asked Adam's birth father for help. She asked him for any kind of help that he could think of, for Adam had trouble forming close relationships with others, trusting others and being honest with others.

Adam's confidence and self-esteem had always been terribly low. Listening to this story, and without wishing to sound melodramatic, I knew his pain. I grew up in the same way, with the same fears, and wished this boy were sitting there with me. I would have hugged him and screamed, 'I know how you feel – you're not alone! What you're feeling is normal and it's OK to feel this. It will get easier and you will work through these feelings in time.' The only advice I had for the birth father was to take his time and allow Adam to set boundaries that he was comfortable with, that Adam would ask for his help and ask the questions he needed to ask when he was ready. In the meantime, just be there for him, do not push him emotionally, never let him down and try to explain why he was given up for adoption and reassure him that it was not because he was not loved or cared for. He was not cast aside as something worthless and unwanted, but was given up to allow him every opportunity, love and a chance at a better life.

At whatever age it dawns on an adopted child, the understanding of adoption can be very painful, especially if their feelings are suppressed. More often than not, they are in fact denied, until such a time as an 'Aidan Murphy' has the courage and love for the adopted person to pick up a mirror and force them to look into it honestly for the first time in their lives. Eventually, the need to search out answers for questions like; was there something wrong with me, am I not worthy of love, need to be answered.

I believe these questions do cross every adopted child's mind. I have heard the words, 'My child has never wanted to search for his/her birth parents.' Perhaps not, but I am of the opinion and sincerely believe every single child given up for adoption does search for answers to certain questions. Whether they search for their birth parents or not, one question, more often than not, needs eventually to be answered on some level: 'Why was I given up for adoption?' For me, having learned everything about myself since my decision to search, that question needed to be answered for peace of mind and peace of heart.

The decision to search or not is one which each adopted person has to make for themselves, and if they decide to search, they must take that journey themselves. The decision to search for my birth parents changed my life and is one of the hardest things I have ever done on my own.

7

THE REALITY
OF SEARCHING

After four weeks without any contact with Aidan, I got a glimpse of how lost I felt without him in my life. I swallowed my pride and picked up the phone and we began to talk honestly about the previous year. Over the next few weeks, he shared with me how hurt and frustrated he had been feeling and made me face some home truths. He spoke to me with the insight of someone who knew me very well, too well for my liking. Aidan made it clear that he thought looking for my roots, as he put it, could help me with some problems I was having, and he promised me he would be there to help me.

He spoke with such care and obvious concern for me and, while I had yet to make amends for how I had treated him, Aidan was convinced that by searching for my birth mother we would be able to work through any problems we had experienced, in time. He made me realise I had to finally admit something was missing from my life. I needed to face my demons and try to piece together a life in which I could be myself completely, not someone made up of my ideas of what people wanted me to be. I opened my heart and mind to this, and let the floodgates open. My desire to reconnect with my birth mother became a longing to find my whole self. She was part of who I was. I needed to feel complete.

To recover from heartache you have to grieve and accept a loss. That is what I had begun to do. Aidan showed me I had the strength to search for answers and to accept that I had been grieving for the loss of those first six weeks of my life. A mere six weeks, yet that time held some very precious answers for me. Once I accepted this, and with the love of those around me to support me when it got tough, I found that I had the courage to seek out my birth mother.

Writing this, I am acutely aware of other adopted people reading it and, as a result, making the decision to search for their birth mothers. This decision, however much it has helped me, is not one that should be made lightly, because it gives a release to deep, deep feelings that you may not have realised were there. Listen to those who love you and, most importantly, be honest with yourself. You'll know if it's right for you. It is possible to find information and answers to some questions, to which you are entitled, without ever wanting to forge a relationship with a birth mother. You may be content with just a few answers. You may not.

I wish I could say that finding this birth mother and possibly having a relationship, in time, will solve all your issues. But it cannot. The search only starts with that first hello – if you are lucky enough to get that far. What is important is that the search is only the beginning, and while you may certainly be able to gain information that might answer some of your questions, searching for a birth mother will not heal all your emotional wounds. It will only start you on the road to self-discovery.

Don't be afraid of learning about yourself, however. If fear is the only thing keeping you from looking for answers, you may well wake up one day and realise you've missed out on amazing opportunities that could have changed your life, allowing you to learn about yourself and hold your head high. You may realise that you're worth a hell of a lot more than you gave yourself credit for or, like myself, that you can cope with far more and are a far stronger person than you had ever imagined.

I can see now that I trusted Aidan enough to reveal everything about myself to him without fear. A man other than my father had shown me how good love can be and that I needn't fear it. I had accepted that in order to become an independent and happy individual, I was going to have to take a leap of faith and search for my birth mother. It was my decision to make but it was the hardest one of my life. I think it might be similar to someone facing a life-saving operation. You are terrified of what could happen and you will be in the hands of both God and the doctors, but you know that it's your only hope. You've got to take the leap or you might not make it. I took the leap.

From the moment I made the decision to start the search, Aidan thought I should talk to Mum and Dad and let them become a part of the journey with me, to support me, but more importantly to include them in my life. Now I had another decision to make. For so long I had tried to hide from them the depth of my feelings concerning my adoption and how it had affected me for much of my late teens and early twenties. By making the decision to contact the adoption agency with Aidan's help, I had turned to someone else and not allowed Mum and Dad to share my pain. To tell them I was now going to search for my birth mum seemed to me to be very hurtful, as if to say, 'Thanks for everything you've done, and I *do* love you, but that's not enough any more. I need more.' I needed time to try to make sense of my reason for searching, enough to be able to put it into words that would not hurt my family.

So I decided to write the initial letter to the adoption agency and then tell Mum and Dad after I heard some news. I thought to myself, I'll cross that bridge when I come to it. I was trying to avoid hurting them, yet by not telling them about my decision to search and not trusting them enough to understand my need to do so, I probably hurt them more. I did not give them the credit that they deserved. I should have waited and come to terms with my decision and then talked it over with my family, who knew me well, whom

I loved and trusted, for they may have been able to prepare me for what was ahead.

During the weeks and months that followed I tried to understand my reasons for searching. I tried to justify it to myself. I hated to think that others might view me as selfish, but more importantly I worried about what those outside of my family might believe to be my reasons for searching. I needed to figure out how to let them know that it was not because of anything lacking in my family – I just needed some answers.

I could not help imagining what the woman who gave birth to me might be like, it is human nature. First I tried to imagine the circumstances surrounding the decision to give me up for adoption. The list is endless, and it is essential that anyone in the same boat understands that anything is possible.

It's very harsh, but I rarely considered the man who had a part in my creation. For me, he was just a person who donated a piece of what made me, no more. Circumstances were to change my perception of what really happened. And maturity has also shown me that, at times, the birth father is ignored and not viewed in the same light as the birth mother.

I wondered if my birth mother had been young, if her parents knew and what they had been like, where she lived. Scenarios of first or forbidden love came to mind; disturbing worries about the possibility of rape, prostitution or worse were also part of my effort to prepare myself for the unknown. Nobody at the early stages of a search has any idea of what to expect. I was always of the opinion, though it was naïve, that I was given up for adoption because it was best for me, to give me a chance in life that my birth mother could not offer, that perhaps she did not have the ability to support a child. And I always believed that she was alone, unable to deal with the responsibility by herself. I tried to imagine how afraid and frightened she must have felt.

Once concerns of this nature were considered, my thoughts turned to what sort of woman she was today. Was she alive, was she in good health, was she a working woman, was she married and so on. The possibilities of what *could be* are endless. I had two preconceptions always in mind. First that she was on her own and made the best decision with me in mind. Second that she had either passed away or had put the past behind her and had possibly married someone else. Whether her new partner knew or not was a problem for another day. Despite trying to keep an open mind and to not hope for anything in particular, and despite the wise words offered by Aidan about trying not to build my hopes up, I had formulated these ideas unconsciously.

Not only this, but I had even harboured an impression of what *sort* of woman she was. I decided that she was more than likely like me, physically and with shared personality traits. She was my birth mother, for God's sake – we had to be very similar, didn't we?

Beware of the way your mind will play tricks on you before you gain any information. You might try hard to take a sensible approach, not to count chickens and not to become too hopeful. For me the truth is that once I admitted my need to search, I began to believe that she had had no choice but to have me adopted, that she was a victim of sorts and that I had to be Christian and caring because of this. I also needed to believe, so badly, that if and when I found her, if I was that lucky (and many are not), we would immediately form a bond. From this bond, and in piecing together the years we had lost, she could solve all my problems. With her answers, she would be able to take away all my hurt, all my pain and make me a new person. All I had to do was be open to it.

The chances of this happening without a rocky road ahead were very slim. I had an ideal of what my birth mother would be like. I had a picture of who I wanted her to be. No mother, nor any daughter, is capable of being the perfect human being. God doesn't make us like that. If you decide to search, take it slow and know that you've a long road ahead and it's probably going to be a bumpy one in places.

Eventually, one night at home after dinner with Mum and Dad, about eight weeks after I had sent that first letter to the adoption society, I told them about my decision. I had had a hard week at work and I was very tired. My emotions always run high when I'm tired and as I sat there, with Mum and Dad chatting, tears started to stream down my cheeks. Mum and Dad asked what in God's name was wrong. After about eight weeks of worrying about what was ahead, I told them about the letter I had sent off to the adoption society. I think they were shocked that I had taken the step to search without letting them know, and while I spent some time trying to reassure them that I loved them as much as ever and trying to explain why I had started this search for my birth mum, they laughed and cried with me.

That night we began to really talk, for the first time about how being adopted had begun to affect me and about what lay ahead for me. I was so overcome with a need to protect them that I didn't realise how this could actually bring us closer in time.

I think Mum had, to some extent, prepared herself for the birth mother being found, whatever the consequences. One step at a time, as they say, and she was at my side at every turn. Dad and Mary were, of course, there to support us both if this birth mother was ever found. We were all guilty of only considering the woman who gave birth to me and anticipating that if I was lucky, we might get to meet her. We ignored the importance of my birth father, or the possibillity that I may also meet him.

Mum, Dad and Mary went through the search experience with me, and each in their own way felt hurt and pain that only they could understand and work through. They tried to ensure that they were always at my side, but still I knew how the search was changing our relationship. It can be a lonely journey at times. Self-doubt haunts you. You needed to do this, in fact every fibre in your being screamed for it, yet you were always aware of those you love and how it was affecting them. For Mum and Dad, earlier in this process, I wonder if they worried that my love for them might be compromised. I am sure it took time for them to accept my reasons for searching.

But there came a time when I simply had to do it: I had to search for my birth mum, for she was the only one who could answer questions for me about those first six weeks, a short few weeks that had in some way moulded the person I had become. To search for her wasn't just a choice or a decision that I made – it was a lifeline that I needed in order to mature and get to know who I was, or rather who I was becoming.

Every adopted person has the right to make this decision, whatever the answers may hold. I have heard some comments over the years on the radio, or in conversation, viewing this choice as selfish, causing unnecessary hurt for those who have loved you all the years they have known you. But the decision to search is not always just from a curiosity to know – sometimes it reaches further and encompasses a need so deep that the decision to search is necessary to become emotionally mature and to learn how to move on with your life, leave the past behind.

One of the truths that you must be aware of, however, when considering whether to search or not, is that adoption does not only affect the adopted person. Its tentacles are unexpectedly far reaching. That is the hardest thing about starting this journey. It will touch not only you, but also those you love. With the best of intentions, and no matter how hard you may try to reassure them, human nature is what it is.

I felt much guilt about my search until Mum and Dad helped me see otherwise. This journey was not so much selfish as necessary for me to grow up to be the person I am today. I hope to be a better daughter, sister and friend because of it. Everyone in my family has been touched by the process of adoption and they have all changed in some way because of it, but I can only hope that it's for the best. Perhaps we are all a little more sensitive, aware of each other's needs, willing to listen and learn from one another. I suppose the day we all feel like we have nothing else to learn is the day that we should just sit by the fireside and give up.

Yes, we have all changed but the biggest transformation has been in myself. Sometimes the people who love me can find it hard to reach me, but someone recently told me that it's getting easier to love me as the days pass, as I let go of much of the anger, resentment and bitterness. They are futile and destructive emotions.

Life is for living and it's a joy to live it. Be honest. Have courage. Forgive. Be open with your feelings and anything is possible.

8

Finding my birth mother ... and a lot more

Once I had made the decision to search, I wrote that first letter to St Patrick's, Haddington Street, Dublin, and explained that the time had come for me to search for my birth mother. I waited each day for the postman, yet I heard nothing for a number of months. I waited and waited. Aidan asked each time we spoke, 'Any news?' I was not even sure whether I was doing the right thing or if I was ready for what I might learn. After I told Mum and Dad, we tried to second-guess what the circumstances might have been surrounding my adoption and tried to prepare for the worst possible outcome. In this way, I believed I could not be hurt. I tried to prepare myself for disappointment.

Two, three, four, then five months passed. I heard nothing and, despite numerous telephone calls to St Patrick's Guild in Dublin, the months turned into a year. I called and left messages again and again. I received no information and often my calls were not taken by the sister in charge. I eventually lost my cool one evening and sat down to write a letter. I told a lie. I wrote that I was engaged and, as the wedding was approaching fast, I really needed to find out if they had any news for me. The wait did one thing only for me: I was now 100 per cent sure that I really did want to have the information they held about my birth mother in the Dublin office. I wasn't sure how I would get it, but I had my mind made up. The staff at St Patrick's were not at all encouraging. In fact, it seemed as if they were trying hard to be evasive each time I spoke with someone.

I had begun to lose patience. I could not understand what could take so long. During that time, I had applied for a job with Jury's Hotels and I had an interview in Dublin. I called the adoption agency a few days before travelling and informed them I would be calling to them and wanted to see someone there about my enquiry. I insisted upon it. I was put on hold and then put through to a nun who told me to bring my passport with me. I enquired why and she told me they would need proof of who I was. I thought it would be a routine meeting, that she might need some information to finish my application – a signature of consent or something similar – and then we could at last start the search properly. I thought nothing more of it and made lunch plans for after the interview.

The day arrived and I went to the interview, met Orla, a good friend, for lunch and told her where I was off to next. She had nothing planned for that afternoon and offered to join me. I was so angry about the delay in gaining any information at all from the agency that Orla wanted to be there for me if I needed a bit of moral support and someone to blow-off steam with afterwards. I thought, why not? I was not prepared for the way that afternoon would unfold.

It should have been handled so much better by the adoption agency. I should have been prepared for the news they were about to deliver. Although the information would have been a shock whenever they gave it to me, I should have had the option to have my family with me to support me. If I had been told that they had some news for me when I called them to inform them of my visit, Mum and Dad would have come with me.

I arrived at the adoption agency, full of the joys. Orla sat downstairs and I was brought upstairs to meet with the sister in charge. The whole meeting only took ten or fifteen minutes. I was told, in very clinical terms, that they had found my birth mother. That in itself was a bombshell. I was then informed, as if she was discussing the weather, that my birth mother had in fact married my birth father, they had seven other children and they all lived in Wicklow. They could not tell me where exactly and said that I could expect the same privacy, but they suggested I write a letter and the agency would forward any correspondence. End of story. I was excused.

When I arrived back downstairs, Orla said I was as white as a sheet. She did not say much but brought me across the road to the pub. She sat me down and ordered me a drink. I told her my news and we both cried. I will never forget her words: 'Typical you, Cashin – Oprah Winfrey here we come!' She was, as always, a rock of sense, with a little pinch of madness to keep a smile on my face. I found a phone immediately and tried Mum and Dad but they were not at home. I cried and told Mary my news and she promised to track them down for me. I left the number of the bar for them to call me back.

After only a few minutes they called me. I could not stop crying. I had planned to stay the night with Orla, but suddenly all I wanted was to get home. It was urgent. I needed to get home to my family, to talk to them about this wonderful, yet terrifying, news. What would this mean? What was going to happen? Orla understood completely and saw me to the train with hugs and words of concern for the journey home. That's the great thing about good friends. You might not see each other that often, or even talk as much as you should, but the friendship is always there. That train journey was the longest of my life – I thought it would never end.

I arrived in Cork train station to see my mum, dad and sister waiting for me. We went to a local pub and sat and laughed and cried. I think I must have been in shock. My heart and mind were racing. I really could not fathom what I had just learned. Thinking back to that night, I really was a young pup of a girl, with no clue about the effect this news was to have on me or what was before me. I called Aidan when I got in and told him the news. He was with his friends Alan and Lucy and, while they were all surprised by the news, they were of course happy for me. I sat at the kitchen table that night and shed tears with my family. I sat on my bed with my mum later that same night and cried until my eyes were dry. I did not know why I was crying.

That was the start of one hell of an emotional roller-coaster. Many times since, I have realised how honest and caring the Wicklow gang have been, even though I have had a lot of trouble dealing with the emotional impact of this new family. But then again, how easy was it for all of them to have to deal with the news of me? I have wondered how they managed to simply accept me as their own, to welcome me as if I had only been away for a while. I hate to think of how I might have reacted if the news had been bad, that my birth mother had died for example, or different in some way, or if these people had wanted nothing to do with me. I wonder how I could have dealt with the knowledge of those people, with exactly the same blood running through their veins, in another part of the country, yet with no contact with them. Things could have been very different and I do realise that I am one of the lucky ones.

The fact that my birth mum and dad had married and had other children, well, that was something that neither I nor my family had considered. The existence of seven siblings was certainly never considered, and this may have been the hardest information for Mary to accept. This search has affected us all and Mary has always found it most difficult and has taken things to heart the most. But we've got to remember that sometimes we have to be a little selfless and think of the needs of others. She knows this and loves me, so everything will be all right, eventually. There are times in your life when you've got to put yourself first and worry about others later, and this was simply one of those times. It sounds harsh, but it is the truth. If I had not found this new family, and without what they have taught me over the past ten years, I would be a very different person: bitter, angry and very much alone, I imagine.

I do wonder how compassionate I would have been in either Mum, Dad or Mary's shoes. It's human nature to feel threatened by those who seem to be competing for the love of someone you cherish. To be quite honest, I don't have the words to describe the confusing emotions that must have wreaked havoc in every one of my family. It takes a pure heart and soul and a lot of love and compassion to put someone else first and to appreciate what they need to feel complete.

Aidan, my husband, was the one who recognised the need for me to search for my birth mother, and he was there to help me deal with what was ahead. These past years have been a time of great self-discovery for me, and the search and every challenge since have affected our relationship and the person I have become. Like most married couples, we have had to overcome certain challenges as husband and wife, but I have also had to take a good look at myself and ask myself what the impact has been on our day-to-day life together.

Getting married at age twenty-five, I was terribly young and naïve and so unprepared for what married life was about. I had a simple view of what a wife should be – traditional in many ways, yet strong and able to deal with what life could throw at her. A lot has changed since that day, much of it because of my search for a birth mother and the confidence this has given me. I also have a better understanding of the pressures on two people who work five days a week and the time that we try to spend together.

In early years of our marriage, I was still used to keeping much of my feelings inside and at bay, controlling any anger and problems I might have. Aidan knew only this facade, for the most part, and had little experience of living with the real me, or the full extent of my feelings. Indeed, I was determined to be a wife that would deliver everything that Aidan wished for. As time passed, I began to experience strong feelings towards the gang in Wicklow. These feelings took control of me and gave me no choice but to deal with them. I could not suppress them, no matter how hard I tried. The ability to deal with my feelings over the years, and the realisation that my feelings were as important as anyone else's, began to seep into my day-to-day pattern of life.

This was to become an issue in my marriage. As I became more comfortable at expressing my feelings and more confident as a person, I found a voice I never realised I had. I was no longer able to accept things just because they were, but understood that if I wanted things to change then I had the right to express this. This cannot have been easy for Aidan. It's difficult marrying one person and learning to live with another. I am a different person and now I am not afraid of what I feel, communicating with others if needs be about what upsets me, and I tend not to bury my head in the sand when someone hurts me. I also have far more self-respect and the voice now to say enough is enough.

Aidan and I have now known each other for over twelve years and both of us are fiery characters – we certainly never hold back when something needs to be aired. People have different priorities and consider different things to be important in a marriage. For me love, trust, fidelity, friendship and valuing each other are some of the most important and vital blocks upon which you can build a good foundation.

With Aidan, anything that happened to shake the trust between us, such a delicate thing at the best of times, was devastating. When at long last I trusted Aidan and let him know my innermost secrets, any betrayal of this set me back years. And when hurt badly, I have always found it difficult to forgive and give someone another chance. Both of these factors can be very destructive forces in any relationship, but especially a marriage, something that is supposed to last a lifetime.

It is your right to know who was responsible for choosing a different life for you and why they decided that was for the best. Aidan has seen a transformation from the Claire who believed she had to be a particular individual to the person I am now. He sat and listened and watched while I cried my heart out, unable to offer the fix I needed, but gave me independent advice and hugs on tap. I am now happy, more carefree and more able to take on life's challenges. I know who I am: someone who does not shy away from life or from people, but who loves a challenge and has begun to live her passions. It can't have been easy for any of them. But they love me and that's what you do for those you love.

I will forever be thankful to my family, to Aidan, to those who love me and to the gang in Wicklow for supporting me in my decision to search and for what came after. They gave me an ear when needed, arms to hold me and understanding at a time that cannot have been easy for them. It is because of these very special people that I had the courage to find the answers that haunted me for many of my younger years.

I can understand why Mary has found this difficult, and as her only sister, I am sure she had worries that we might grow apart. I tried to reassure her at each step of the way. I found myself buying cards that effused love for my sis. I picked up notelets with sentimental verses proclaiming everything our relationship meant to me, how I treasured it and would be lost without it. I still wonder if she truly realises what this search has meant for me. My decision to search was not because of anything lacking in my relationships with my family but because of something lacking in my knowledge of myself, in knowing who I was during those first six weeks of life. It was not a judgement on the way I was loved or raised. It was just the final piece of the puzzle.

The gang in Wicklow, also, this must have been hard for them, especially for my birth mum and birth dad, Mai and Tony. How must it have felt to give up a child for adoption and, having married anyway, to imagine what could have been if they had not made the decision they did? When I try to comprehend how I would have dealt with this loss and how anger might have been a part of their marriage, blaming one another at times, I just cannot grasp what it must have been like.

At times, Aidan and I are guilty of blaming each other for something stupid, like who did not feed the cat before we left for work. How must Mai and Tony have blamed each other in those earlier years? I cannot begin to understand how this has shaped them and haunted them? How did the news of this new 'sister' affect the rest of their children – to learn that there was another girl in Cork, who shared the same blood, yet they knew nothing about me? That must have been hard also.

One of my friends, Rachael, has been affected too, I am sure of it. It's not something we talk very much about but a few months back she read the preface to this book and, despite an initial lack of words and surprise, her hug and tears spoke a thousand wise words. Her experience has been very different and witnessing the other side of the coin cannot have been easy. I have family members who have also experienced adoption and knowing the way my story unfolds may have seemed surreal and difficult not to compare to their own experience. Imagine if things had been different for Mai? If she and Tony had not married or if another spouse had to be told about a daughter who had come looking for them.

A birth mum must always have an awareness of their adopted child out there somewhere, yet simply knowing about them surely cannot prepare you for your feelings if this child were ever to search you out. If Mai had married someone else, would her husband have been able to accept me for Mai's sake, for the sake of the love that he had for her? No scenario is easy and I'm trying to convey to any adopted person who is reading this book that your decision will have consequences for everyone. This is not your fault: it is a fact that because you were given up for adoption, if you decide to search in later years you will face challenges. What lies ahead can be downright hard and it takes so much time, talking, tolerance, love and understanding from anyone who has been touched by the process.

Aidan and I shared a boozy night with Rachael and David recently. Rachael happens to be married to David, Aidan's best friend. David, out of love for Rachael, expressed his concern over this book. He worried that people might not understand my need to write this book. He understood that my 'story' had it all, the perfect scenario. Didn't they marry and after time didn't we sort everything out and were now forming relationships with one another? He wondered how hard it might be for others who were not so lucky to read about such a happy tale, that it might be difficult for them.

I know that there are adopted people in the world who have not been as lucky as me. I can understand what he was saying, but it's like anything else in life – you never know what goes on behind closed doors and maybe each scenario depends on each person and their ability to deal with things. Aidan tried to explain to him that, although, yes, the initial news was happy and I was indeed very blessed, there were aspects of this revelation that were very hard to accept and that I had demons of my own to fight still.

I know what David was trying to say. This book does tell the story of a new-found birth family in Wicklow, but more importantly it tells of how hard confronting the issues surrounding adoption can be. While the story shows how lucky I am, I have tried to write about what I have learned and how each adopted person will learn lessons that will be difficult and some of the challenges may at times seem insurmountable. But it can be done: you can overcome anything that life throws at you. It's a state of mind. It is about approaching life knowing how much you are willing to achieve and how much you are willing to change and accept.

I do know this much: no one can do it alone and you need to be man or woman enough to admit when you need someone to lean on. It's a slow process and should be a gradual one, progressing when you are ready for the next little step. To start a search or not, that is something that only you can decide, and you will need to be able to look deep inside your own heart.

When I first learned about this new birth family in Wicklow, I had a plan of action all thought out. I knew what I wanted to do and how it was all about to happen. But the way things eventually panned out, I really hadn't planned for any of it *at all*.

9

A JOURNEY STARTS WITH JUST ONE STEP

Having received the news from the adoption agency, those first few weeks in September, I naïvely believed that the hardest part was over. I knew Mai was alive and I also knew now that my birth father, Tony, was alive. I would not have to face the possibility that my birth mother had died, which would have left me unable to get any answers for the questions I had begun to ask. Mai and Tony had married, they had a family of their own, seven other children, and the nun had told me that Mai in particular really wanted to hear from me, so I assumed that she wanted me to become a part of their lives. When I began the search, I considered the hardest part to be the possibility of rejection, but now that they wanted to hear from me, which eliminated this fear. The only thing for me to decide now was what to say in my very first letter to my natural birth parents, Mai and Tony.

Looking back on that time and those few days before I sent off my first letter to them, it strikes me as strange that I was so trusting of them. The only things I knew about them were their names, where they lived and how many children they had. Up until then, I had been afraid of any new situation in my life, wary of people I did not know, and I tried to second-guess people's motives where possible. So why I trusted Mai and Tony from the moment I heard about them and ventured gung-ho into our potential relationship to this day astounds me. Perhaps it was because of my initial relief that they were married to each other and so I would not have to be kept a secret from another husband. Maybe I wished, and so made myself believe, that because Mai and I were connected by blood, after all she carried me for nine months, we would, of course, connect. How could we not?

Writing that first letter, I sat at the table in my bedroom for what seemed like ages before I had any idea what to write. I started that letter the morning after I returned from Dublin and it took me three days, writing and rewriting it, before I was happy with what it said. It had to be perfect, I remember thinking to myself, 'What exactly am I supposed to say to the people who were responsible for bringing me into this world, yet are strangers to me? Hi, my name is Claire. This is my life and I'm terrified you won't like me?'

The first piece of advice I can give to anyone who finds themselves in the same shoes is just be yourself. Don't say anything you believe you *should* say or that you don't genuinely feel. I tried so hard to find the right words and I wanted my letter to be special. I actually wanted approval from them, so I tried to make sure the letter I sent to them initially was *right*. I wanted them to think I was a nice person, a caring person, someone they would want to become part of their lives. Again, I tried to please them and, while everything in the letter was true, my words avoided the very questions I wanted to scream at them, 'Why did you give me up for adoption when you married anyway?'

I had left Cork for Dublin that Friday morning without any real concerns and by Saturday I had been told that Mai and Tony had married a year after I was adopted. I remember that Saturday like it was yesterday, wanting to write words that would be welcomed by them, yet already beginning to feel a deep-seated anger creep into my heart because they had married one another. My previous fantasy of Mai had led me to weave a picture of her as a helpless woman on her own, with no choice but adoption for me. But I still wanted them to think I was a nice person. I wanted them to like me, and so I hid all the emotions that began to build inside me from them. I didn't want to frighten them away now. The pattern of my inner beliefs set in: if they saw what I was thinking or could see the person I really was, then they would reject me.

Here's my second piece of advice; I was given these words of wisdom not once but many times by people much wiser than me, because they loved me. Take your time! Do not rush the process. I wanted to send the letter immediately; I wanted to receive a reply immediately. I wanted to meet them, to see them straight away. Did we look alike? Would they fall madly in love with me? Would we connect with one another on some level? I had waited over twenty years for this happy news and I wanted it all to happen – now! Mum and Dad stood by, watching and waiting helplessly, trying to protect me, but would I listen? Not a hope – there was a better chance of hell freezing over! I am a stubborn person at the best of times and once my mind is made up, that's that, done and dusted. I rushed the letter off, and so it didn't really represent the real me. I wrote a letter full of the joys and tried to tell them as much as I could about my life and the family I loved so much. I took out the photo albums with Mum and Dad and chose some pictures to go with this letter.

From the moment that first letter was posted, I awoke every morning before the postman arrived and ran downstairs the minute I heard the latch on the gate opening. I was still living at home and Mum and Dad kept a close eye on me while I waited for a reply. They kept saying, 'This has been a huge shock for you.' I thought, 'What's the big deal? Things are fine. Look how things have turned out – things are great. Relax!' But parents really have the market cornered when it comes to being wise and knowing what's best for their children. We talked and laughed and joked about what little information I had gained, until one day, about two weeks later, a letter arrived, registered.

I ran upstairs to Mum and Dad's room, sat on the bed and read eagerly. Mai had also enclosed some photographs for me. We looked again and again at the photographs and letter. I was staring at the two people who had given me my nose, my hair, my everything *physically*. It was so strange. I think it was then that the wonderful news began to sink in. I walked around on air for a number of days and carried Mai's first letter with me everywhere. I had aunts calling, close friends of the family, buddies of my own, cousins, and even then I did not appreciate how excited and flabbergasted everyone would be that Mai and Tony had actually married.

A few more letters passed between us and we gained more information about one another. Mai and Tony learned about my family and upbringing and I in turn learned about their life in Wicklow – well, as much as we could learn from letters. They were farmers who not only had a large family themselves, but also were blessed with a large extended family. I learned that I had seven brothers and sisters, aged at that stage from nineteen down to one. I looked at every physical aspect of the people who stared back at me from the photographs and immediately some similarities were obvious.

Again, the impact this might have on my life began to hit home. I wanted to be a part of their lives, of course, very much so, and yet I wasn't sure what was going to happen, or more importantly *how* it was going to happen. One thing I did learn from some of Mai's first letters was that she thought it best to wait before telling her gang about me. Common sense led me to understand what Mai was saying to me, that they had raised their family up until now doing their best to teach them certain moral lessons. For her to have to turn around and tell them all, especially the older ones, 'By the way, we actually had a baby *before* we were married and we gave her up for adoption' would be a difficult thing to do. While

I understood this, it was still hard to be the person who had to be kept secret. I thought that as they had married there would be no reason to hide or feel ashamed of what had happened all those years ago. Mum kept trying to help me to understand Mai's viewpoint, being a mother herself, but it was a difficult thing to come to terms with.

Reason told me that there were things Mai and I needed to do first and that we needed to take things one step at a time. We still had to meet. September, October and November passed and I received my first Christmas card from Mai and Tony that December. We exchanged letters every few weeks, and after a couple of months I began to grow tired of the wait between letters so I sent a letter to the adoption agency giving permission for Mai to write to me at home, and so we started to correspond directly. After only a short time, it became evident that we were both growing impatient and couldn't wait any longer for our first meeting. Our letters up to this point were very much about our day-to-day lives. Mai kept me informed about her gang and who was up to what, but neither of us had yet expressed anything of an emotional nature. She tried her best to explain by letter why the decision to have me adopted had been made, but letters by that stage were not enough.

We decided to arrange our first meeting in early March 1997, a few weeks before my birthday. Mai and Tony and I arranged to meet halfway, in a hotel in Waterford, mid-afternoon on a Saturday. I made some decisions regarding this meeting that might have been difficult for Mum and Dad to accept initially. It was not an easy time for them – a fact I was never allowed to see or to worry about, I might add. They hid any concerns about themselves and their role as my mum and dad from me. Despite constantly telling me that they were, of course, delighted with my meeting Mai and Tony and knew I would always love them as Mum and Dad, I knew they still needed reassurances.

I thought long and hard about what was about to happen and I was terrified. I was worried about meeting Mai and Tony and also very conscious of not hurting Mum and Dad and ensuring they knew that the meeting had nothing to do with the bond we shared. But I worried about how Mum and Dad would feel if I cried when I met Mai and Tony or if I wanted to hug them. What if we hit it off - would that be hard for Mum and Dad to witness? If my parents were also there, it would be obvious to Mai and Tony how close we were - would that make them very sad or uncomfortable or maybe make them hold back when we met? Worrying about the dynamics of two sets of parents, along with my own fears, was enough to nearly send me over the edge. Aidan and I had since become engaged; we had done a lot of talking and managed to resolve the problems we had been having. I made my mind up that it was going to be hard enough meeting Mai and Tony without worrying about anyone else, so I asked Aidan to come with me instead of Mum and Dad. After all, he had seen the worst of me and what better person to be there to hold my hand? It had been his idea to start the ball rolling after all.

I was happy yet terrified the Friday night before the meeting, and so I met Aidan to calm my nerves. That particular Friday evening, however, my parents sat at home, waiting with my favourite dinner in the oven, worrying about where I could be. They needed so much to be involved and included in how this was affecting me. I was very late home and did not give them the opportunity to share my fears and worries. They were a part of my life up until then, and at that point I did not include them. This was not a conscious decision – it was a protective mechanism kicking in. If you don't feel it, it doesn't exist. If you don't show how much this means to you, then you can't hurt Colum and Eileen. No matter how hard I tried to keep my emotions hidden from them, however, they knew that something was making me very unhappy.

They *were* with me in my heart the next day, but it really was a little easier for me to do it 'alone'. A rugby match was on the television, as if it were just another day. Dad suggested we sit and watch it for a while, trying, I think, to delay what would be a tough day for me. But I needed to be on my way. I can't imagine what those hours were like for them, sitting at home, worrying about me. I think they understand it all now, though. At least, I hope they do.

They had envisioned that first meeting between Mai and Tony and myself at home in Cork, over a few drinks, and maybe taking out the photo albums, but Mai and Tony were not comfortable with this suggestion. It was easier for us all to meet on neutral ground. One day, a few weeks before that first meeting, Dad had me in stitches. The time was drawing near and I was really uptight and he could see it. We were sitting outside, enjoying the spring sunshine, and he said, quite seriously, 'I have a great idea, we can root out Claire's communion dress, her confirmation dress, get her debs dress out of storage and put on a fashion show for Mai and Tony – better than a photo album any day!' I nearly cracked up laughing. To laugh from the bottom of my heart like that was much needed. It was a reminder of the happy occasion that was soon to take place and not to worry so much about it. Mai, Tony and myself had the same blood running through us, didn't we? Things couldn't go that wrong.

That Saturday in March arrived all too soon. I had slept no more than one hour the night before and I get unfortunate dark shadows under my eyes when I don't sleep. I also had a bad hair day, and when you have very curly hair that's really a sight to be seen. My hands wouldn't stop shaking. I had been sick at 8 a.m. and again at 9. I didn't say much that morning. I got dressed, after finally deciding what to wear – what exactly are you supposed to wear when meeting your birth parents for the first time? I told everyone I loved them and that I would call them the minute I could.

Aidan and I were to stay the night in Waterford after meeting Mai and Tony. He arrived and we started on our way. It must have been a nice change for him – I didn't say much!

About half an hour into the journey, I asked to stop at a bar. I had two vodka and Diet Cokes. Half an hour later and we were on the road again. By 12.30 p.m. we stopped again and had another two drinks and a bite to eat. Aidan ate most of my food. I can't quite remember, but I think I may have been sick again. By about 2 p.m., we had arrived in the hotel bar in Waterford. I walked around trying to see which seats would have a view from every angle, so I could spot Mai and Tony before they saw me. Eventually I gave up and just sat down and had another vodka and Diet Coke. By 3 p.m. my hands were wet, my bladder had been drained so many times I thought I might have had an infection and my tongue was stuck to the roof of my mouth. Was I mad? My mind screamed 'run', but my heart insisted I stay.

3.05 p.m. The moment had arrived. Before I had a chance to look up and focus, I saw a bear of a man come towards me with arms outstretched and pull me into one of the biggest hugs I have ever had in my life. I pulled back and saw Mai, a small woman who was obviously as terrified as me. I gave her a kiss and we all sat down. It is surreal to finally sit across the table from the two people you would have called Mum and Dad had circumstances been different, having imagined this moment, or something like it, for most of your life. I knew Eileen and Colum Cashin as Mum and Dad and loved them as such – nothing would change that, ever. But now I could touch this man and woman sitting across from me, who were, by birth, my mum and dad, and yet they were complete strangers.

We shared some small pieces of information in the few hours we spent together. Tony could not stop looking at me while I spoke with Mai. I suppose it was strange for them to see certain similarities with the gang at home. I found this attention hard to deal with. While I was deliriously happy to meet them and would hopefully get to know them in time, Mai and Tony seemed to have a sense of relief that at last I was back in their life. This made me feel very afraid. I was unsure of what they expected from me. We sat and chatted and I answered as many questions as I could. Aidan said that it was amazing to see the similarities between the three of us. However, now our relationship had progressed another step, and I had yet to realise that we had to establish boundaries and a pace we were *all* comfortable with.

It was just all so strange. While I sat there with them, looking at every feature, trying to notice similarities, my mind would not stop racing. I tried hard to concentrate on the words being spoken around me, but I was so in awe of the situation I found myself in, that there were times I just had to smile at the right time and try and switch off the bedlam inside my head. I remember Tony was determined to make sure we had enough to eat, or drink, and anything we needed, I needed especially, was provided for. He rushed to the bar insisting he pay for the drinks we ordered, he raced ahead of Aidan to pay for the sandwiches. When we settled in our seats and I began to relax a little the situation became a little more comfortable for us all and Aidan and I began to enjoy our few drinks. I could see Tony watching this and a look of concern crossed his face. He asked us if we wanted some tea or coffee and we said we were grand. A few minutes passed and he again suggested getting tea and coffee but none of us wanted any. Mai laughed and told him to stop fussing. One last offer of tea or coffee and when we said no thanks, he mentioned that maybe with a long drive ahead of us back to Cork it would be no harm to have a quick cup. The penny dropped- he was worried that we would be getting into the car with a few drinks under our belt! We all laughed and explained that Aidan and I had booked into the hotel for the night and there was no need to worry about drinking and driving. Their concern was so genuine and I smiled to myself, they were worried about me already.

I was overjoyed with how the day had gone. When it was time for them to start the journey home, we hugged and promised to keep in close contact. I had done it. We had met and it was onwards and upwards from there. I remember standing there, watching them walk out the door and even though I knew this first meeting had gone well, I suddenly felt afraid of what would happen next. We promised to call and continue to write letters, but what guarantee was there that there would be more contact? What happened if … Again I was jumping ahead instead of just enjoying the moment and the first hurdle we had overcome.

But the worry was fleeting. Aidan turned to me and just hugged me without any words being spoken. There was no need to say anything until I was ready. How do you find the words to describe such a life-changing moment? An emotion so electrifying and pure that it must have been joy or elation coursing through my body. I had found a peace of sorts. I immediately went upstairs to phone Mum and Dad. I cried with them and, between gulps of air, told them everything.

I went back downstairs to Aidan and we drank until the wee hours of the morning. A weight had lifted from my shoulders, a weight that had been sitting there for quite a number of years. Mai had tried to explain why they had decided to give me up for adoption, but we had yet to explore some very deep feelings we had both held onto for so long. Mai had felt huge guilt for having had me adopted, and my own feelings about the fact that they had married still had to find their way to the surface. My abiding memory from that day is Tony's words, and they were heartfelt. Mai became very emotional at one stage and excused herself for a breath of fresh air. Tony told us that in all their years of marriage this was the first time he had ever really heard Mai speak at length about the baby they had given up for adoption. More importantly, it was perhaps the first time she had revealed the true depth of her emotions and worries about me during the years. To say it was a very emotional day for us all does not do those hours justice. That meeting with Mai and Tony will always be one of the most rewarding experiences of my life.

We returned to normal living and continued to write directly to one another. Now I had time to think about what had happened since I had learned about the gang in Wicklow and to try to feel comfortable about the feelings that had begun to surface. I fear that my words now might not properly convey my feelings at that time. Mai and Tony are genuine people and have been very loving and understanding. They have welcomed me into their family, in a way in which I could not have dreamed of in a thousand years. Still, certain thoughts came and settled; I had made my mind up about a few things, and no one was about to change my mind.

I read a novel recently about a brother and sister who were adopted and the counsellor in this book made a comment that struck a chord. She said to the young girl that she felt two types of adoptees went looking for their birth parents: those who wanted to and those who *needed* to. She finished this statement with the belief that it is better to be someone who wanted to. Having experienced the process, I believe I was someone who needed to. I was having difficulties with being an adopted child and needed to find out why I was given up for adoption. I think, without realising it, that I particularly wanted to hurt Mai for having hurt me by placing me for adoption all those years ago. I *needed* to find her to be able to work through my emotions.

Mai and Tony had told me that they were young, in their early twenties and that, as Tony had broken his leg and couldn't get a job at the time, marriage and the ability to support a child were out of the question. So I was given up for adoption. I can understand the logic behind that, and I realise that I was loved enough for them to want me to have a good life, with everything that had to offer. But nine years ago, around the time of our first meeting, all I could understand was, 'You broke your leg and yet within the year you married anyway and began to start your family. Why couldn't you have fought for me? Why couldn't you have loved me enough to want me to be yours?' I never said this to either of them, yet I harboured these feelings, and they ate away at me. These destructive emotions changed my personality for a while, and I didn't forgive them for a number of years. While I am not by nature a hurtful person, my emotions at that time got the better of me and I was unable to stop myself lashing out and hurting others.

Now, I have the maturity to understand that they were hurting for far longer than I was, with the uncertainty of never knowing if I was all right. I still am bitter towards the institutions, Catholic mostly at that time, who claim to be Christian and doing the work of God. Mai contacted the adoption society many times over the years, simply to know if I was all right, and they told her again and again that they could not give her any information – not even to put her heart and mind at rest. When I was born, Mai purchased a little jacket for me and when I was whisked away, because Mai was not allowed to see me, she asked the nun could she leave this little outfit with me. This Christian woman, with God as her witness, provided no reassurances that I would have this jacket to keep and know that it was from my birth mother. Was she not entitled to some compassion from that nun? I never received the jacket nor, more importantly, the knowledge that she had wanted me to have it.

After meeting Mai and Tony, our letters became increasingly frustrated and less able to describe the spectrum of feelings we were both experiencing. Each time either Mai or myself stated something in a letter to the other, we seemed to misunderstand what was meant, and anger and confusion began to grow. Mai did not like writing letters and suffered from arthritis, while I hated to speak on the phone, her preferred medium of communication. I couldn't pop up for coffee, as the kids didn't yet know, so we muddled along as best we could. Neither of us seemed to be any good at expressing ourselves during this time. I think the deplth of our feelings smothered us and our ability to talk with one other.

I don't want to hurt Mai and Tony with my words and the following explanation is merely what *I believed* Mai was trying to convey to me at that time, a time when I was very emotional and sensitive about everything. From the depth of feeling and honesty in Mai's letters, it seemed as if she believed that at last there was someone she could talk to about giving me up for adoption, that we could become friends and share information openly, but I was barely able to do this with Aidan, never mind a woman who, in reality, I did not know or, more importantly, did not trust yet. I began to feel under pressure and started to panic. At that time, I felt I couldn't be her long lost daughter. I didn't know how to offer love to someone who was still a stranger to me. I was unsure what was expected of me and, as time passed, I began to feel angry that the rest of the family still did not know about me. It doesn't matter how long that took. What *does* matter, however, is that I was not mature enough to be willing to try and understand Mai's situation.

The facts are clear, yet not simple, for how can words really describe the emotions that must have eaten away at Mai over the years? Mai became pregnant in a rural area, at a time in Ireland when it was considered shameful to be unmarried and pregnant. Many girls in Mai's situation were sent away 'to an aunt' or some family member during the course of their 'confinement' to avoid the community finding out. Holy Catholic Ireland was not a forgiving or understanding place, and I think Mai felt she would hurt those near and dear to her and disappoint them terribly if she were to reveal the truth. So the decision was made to have me adopted. I don't know what conversations Mai has had with her family, her own brothers, since news of me broke or how hurt they may have felt at not having known about me all those years. I think if I learned my sister had had to bear such heartache all her life because she felt she could not tell me, I would feel hurt. Mai said to me recently that now she knows that her mum, dad and brothers would have supported her, but hindsight is a wonderful thing. But it doesn't do us any good to cry over what could have been. Over the years I have shed too many bitter tears thinking of that.

I eventually sent one of her letters back to Tony, asking him to please help Mai. I told him that I could not continue until such a time as I did not feel under so much pressure. I was confused and afraid and unsure of what to do. Mai had stated in that last letter that she felt as if I only wanted her to tell the kids, that I had no real interest in her or Tony. I didn't know what to say to that. It simply wasn't true. I went looking for her and no one else. In the letter I sent to Tony with her last letter, I tried to explain how I found Mai's emotions very difficult to deal with. I was finding my own hard enough, never mind trying to fathom Mai's and how to help her with them.

I did not receive a reply from either Mai or Tony and there were no further letters or contact from them for a number of years, as I had asked. It's just as well, as I was unable to cope with anything for a while, until I came to terms with my own feelings. Mai and I did our best during that year to try and understand one another but we were both wrapped up in our own emotions. I cannot write about how Mai must have felt at this time, for she does that far better in a later chapter. For now, I can only explain what I felt.

Now, I feel regret at the mess Mai and I made of things. We can look back now at that time and smile at what happened between us. We are both alike in many ways – stubborn to the core. For my part in the breakdown of communication, I need to admit to some things, and although they might be understandable under the circumstances, the way I felt and the manner in which I reacted to these feelings had a direct impact on how slowly we got to know one another. I handled things badly.

When we met for the first time, I found the immediate physical contact very difficult to deal with – the hugs, the little touch to my hand and the strength and openness from Mai and Tony was very hard to accept. Like myself, they were happy to finally have the chance to meet, yet I was used to being more reserved with people I did not know. That's the truth of the situation: we did not know one another and to hear from Mai, and especially Tony, from very early on that they loved me was something I was not used to. Anyone who knows me might find that strange because I am usually an expressive person, very quick to hug and proclaim my fondness and love for family and friends. But I only feel comfortable with a show of affection like this either from or towards people I know very, very well. After that meeting, things progressed quickly. We no longer just corresponded by letter. Now I was receiving telephone calls at home, but I could not call them at their home, as the kids did not know about me yet. It seemed as if our budding relationship was to some extent controlled by Mai and Tony. I felt I was at their mercy and I found that hard to handle.

While I could understand the torment and guilt that Mai evidently felt at having lost the years between us and at the loss, to some extent, of a child, I also found her openness and honesty very hard to take. I was delighted that she finally had someone she felt she could share the pain of those lost years with, but I still had much to try and understand myself and found juggling the two very painful indeed. I tried to help Mai in my own way by listening to her and offering advice where I could, but I began to feel angry and I had many questions that needed answers. However, it seemed that the time was never right and I did not wish to burden her with them. So I kept quiet, until my feelings found an escape in my letters to her. While I still had not expressed my anger to Mai and Tony concerning their marriage shortly after my adoption, I am sure that this was what fed my emotions in those early years in our relationship.

I had yet to forgive Mai for giving me up to be adopted and that was something I had never considered to be a problem. I had always thought I only ever felt gratitude towards my birth mum for giving me the Cashin name and a happy upbringing, yet when I stopped to really think about what I was feeling, the truth of the matter was that I wanted to show her what the pain of growing up had been like for me. I wanted her to know what it felt like to be hurt by your own flesh and blood. I had no control over these emotions – they just came in waves so strong they nearly took my breath away. At very ordinary moments in my day-to-day life, while doing the washing up or changing the sheets, my mind would wander, and I simply had to stop what I was doing and allow the tears and anger to happen, to come and envelop me until I was able to continue.

When Mai and I talked, I also began to feel disturbed about what I understood as her feelings towards my Mum and Dad. Even though Mum and Mai talked for a few moments on the phone whenever she called, and Mai often asked me how they were doing, I got the impression that they were only interested in getting to know me and were excluding Mum and Dad to some extent from my new life with them. I became fiercely protective of Mum and Dad and again became angry with Mai and Tony over this. My life was in Cork with my family and I needed them to know that nothing, absolutely nothing, would ever change that. I felt sorry that this was the reality of the situation, but nothing could take back the years. Looking back now, however, I can see that I was over-sensitive about everything. Mai had to try to learn about me first. There was time enough for everything else later.

That first year we made contact, it was a little easier to be patient about the rest of the family knowing about me. But as time passed, it became harder for me to wait, knowing about them all and the paths their lives had taken, yet not being able to become a part of their lives. I felt angry about this, and Mai must have felt my impatience and anger. This led her to believe that I only wanted to form bonds with the rest of the family and not with her, an assumption that was alien to me. Needless to say, this also added fuel to the fire.

In the past, I have rarely had the confidence to mark out boundaries for others, or to indicate what makes me feel uncomfortable. I did not feel comfortable telling people in plain English what I wanted, finding it much easier to try and deliver what I thought *they* wanted. So I never asked Mai and Tony to stop doing or saying certain things. I'm sure they believed that I was happy with the way things were going because I did not do anything to make them believe otherwise in that first year. I was afraid of doing something that would push them away. Everything began to build up and my ability to understand anything or get things back on track, in a way that I was comfortable with, seemed too hard a task. It was easier to lash out, put a stop to the relationship and call it quits. Things were going far too quickly for me to handle. I needed out.

I led everyone to believe that this was what I wanted, that I was happy with the lack of contact and that it was for the best. I think I was trying to protect myself. It seemed to me that I could not even have a conversation with this woman who was essentially my mother. The immediate bond that I had longed for just didn't seem to exist. Although Mum and Dad seemed to be handling this turn of events in my life reasonably well, Mary was having difficulty in accepting my choice and I was sorry I had hurt her. But Mum and Dad stood silently by and tried to support my decision. Although they tried to prompt discussions about what had happened and to get me to explore my feelings, they knew when not to push me. They tried to help me to understand the pain that Mai must have experienced through the years and to give it time.

I tried to get on with my life and put it all out of my mind. It was easier said than done. But as with many other issues in my life, Mum and Dad knew all along that things weren't quite finished with, not yet, despite what I kept trying to tell myself.

10

BLOOD IS THICKER
THAN WATER

I tried to continue with the day-to-day aspects of my life and I told myself that I wasn't missing out on much – after all, what I never had, I wouldn't miss. I was working in a solicitor's office in Cork and I had a wedding to organise. While I accepted what had happened between Mai and I, I was still disappointed with the way things had gone. But I was never a quitter and I knew deep down that I had not seen this to the end, not yet. I also knew that I had to accept responsibility for the way I had reacted to Mai, but at this early stage of our relationship I was incapable of being honest with myself. I was devastated that the bond I had imagined we would share was not immediate and it seemed that she was just like the rest of us. She was a woman who was not able to take away my pain simply by virtue of having given birth to me. The dream gave way to reality in the cold light of day. I was also terrified that she would realise that I too was very ordinary, nothing exceptional, and so might decide that sorting out the mess would not be worth the trouble. So I reacted in a way that was comfortable and familiar to me: I cut my losses before she could hurt me.

Mum and Dad tried to draw me out and get me to talk about what had happened, and while they could understand why I had made the decision to leave well enough alone, they also tried to make me see it from Mai's perspective and forgive what I needed to forgive. I learned a lot about people during this time in my life, and many might disagree with some of the things I am about to say, but these are my experiences, so I know them to be very real and overpowering. I learned quickly that people, without first-hand knowledge of what adoption means, can be quick to judge and to judge me. I once overheard someone, who really didn't know me well at all, say, 'I don't know why she ever felt she had to go looking for her birth mother. She's so lucky to have parents like Colum and Eileen. Why is she doing this?'

It was as if some people believed I owed something to Mum and Dad. I actually believed this myself for many years, until they showed me otherwise. Yes, I owed them my love, as any other child would, but should I feel grateful to them for rescuing me from something for the rest of my life? Mum and Dad have always told me they are thankful for the gift of me and for the happiness I brought to their lives. But the point is that this person expected me to be forever grateful. Questioning whether this debt will ever be paid is a heavy weight.

I went looking for the woman who gave birth to me because she was the only one who could answer my questions and fill in those first few weeks before I became adopted. Whether I wanted to admit it or not, those six weeks had left a void in my life, and I needed information about that time so I could become complete and move on with my life. Some part of me, deep down, had stopped the journey I had begun in order to conform in some way to what other people judged as the right thing to do. Coupled with this was the terror I had felt at what I believed to be the beginning of rejection for the second time in my life from the same woman. In kicked my protective mechanism from years past – reject Mai before she could reject me.

I was dealing with things as best I could. I was aware that the safe way in which I had led my life, until meeting Mai and Tony, was over. The moment I admitted to myself I had certain issues to deal with as a result of being adopted, my control over my emotions was relinquished, and not by choice. Mai and Tony had become a part of my life, however small, and they had the ability to dash my hopes and crush me, if I allowed it. I considered myself lucky to have gone so far, and now I had some of the answers to the initial questions that had been unanswered for over twenty years, such as what sort of a woman my birth mother was, and the circumstances surrounding my adoption. So why, I asked myself, was I not content with this?

One weekend shortly before Aidan and I were to be married, I was on my own, as Mum and Dad were away for the weekend, and I felt desperately alone. I have heard many other stories from adopted people my own age about this time in their lives: when they were due to be married, a new start, a new life, and their need at that particular juncture to search out their birth mothers. I had an empty space in my heart that seemed to ache every time I thought about Mai and Tony and what had gone wrong. It's a very destructive thing to know exactly *what* is upsetting you, without perhaps understanding the true depth of your feelings, and not wanting to admit it to anyone. I hated the thought of being in any way vulnerable. I started to cry early one evening, and for the first time, on my own, I let my emotions flow. And that moment I realised that the time had come to finally have the courage to examine my true feelings. I needed to talk to someone, and quickly.

I picked up the phone and called Mum's sister Marie, and for that half hour I will always be thankful. I knew I had to sort things out quickly, because I was having problems pretending I was happy to leave well enough alone. Marie soothed me and basically told me everything I was feeling was normal under the circumstances. She didn't make me feel selfish for wanting to find my birth mother or stupid for crying like a helpless child. Mum and Dad didn't make me feel this way either, but they were tied closely to this search and my own worries about hurting them were eating away at me.

Marie suggested that speaking to someone experienced in matters of adoption might be helpful. I asked her to look into it for me and slept soundly that night for the first time in a long while. Marie called me the next day and arranged everything for me. I felt such relief when I woke up that morning, having shared the burden of my guilt about believing that I had hurt my family, and having shared my sheer desperation at being unable to make sense of conflicting emotions where Mai was concerned. I needed her to accept me, yet I shut her out. I wanted to get to know her family, yet I was terrified that they would not accept me. Deep down, I wanted so much to become part of this new birth family, yet I did not want my family in Cork to feel hurt because of this need.

Despite the relief that day, I was fearful of how Mum and Dad might react to the news that Marie was arranging for me to see someone professionally. I felt embarrassed about talking to someone who dealt with people with emotional problems, a shrink of some sort. While it had become evident that I was unable to make sense of so many emotions on my own, that I was utterly confused and unable to decide what I really wanted, I still did not want anyone to think I was 'sick', that my mind was not right in some way. After all, I was normal – wasn't I?

Until that moment, I had not had much experience of suiting myself when it came to important decisions in my life. But now I was facing a very real decision: whether to try and get to know Mai and give her a chance. And this decision was one I had to make for myself, without any thought for others I cared about. Because this was something that was going to affect me for the rest of my life.

I remember having to ask Lucia, my boss at that time, for an hour off here and there during work hours and having to explain about the counselling and why this was so important for me. Outside of the family, this was the first time I had had to reveal the difficult well of emotions within me and I felt terribly vulnerable and embarrassed. I shed a few tears but Lucia smiled and reassured me that this was no problem at all – she said she thought that it was a really good idea and that I was lucky. She made me feel it was all right to need this and made it very easy for me, like it was no big deal.

So I began to meet with a counsellor every two weeks or so. Having the opportunity to talk to someone who was not connected to anyone in my life allowed me to speak openly about how I was really feeling. Feelings of despair and joy, of terror and excitement, of guilt and expectancy. This counsellor told me, though not in so many words, that I could say anything in that room, that nothing was taboo and that I was not going to hurt anyone by being honest with myself. She showed me that if I could learn to become honest with myself between those four walls, then I might learn what I really wanted and bring this truth to my life outside of my relationship with her. Yes, she *was* a counsellor, but she was just a woman who went to college to learn how to do her job properly. Just like I did, just like an accountant does, just like many people do – yet we don't feel embarrassed at needing the services of a mechanic because they might know more about cars than we do. This woman just knew more about how to deal with the workings of my mind for a time, until I allowed myself to listen to my own needs, hidden deep down.

So, when I told Mum and Dad about Marie's suggestion, they welcomed the chance for me to talk to anyone – to the pope if it would help – in order for me to figure out the path I would choose and to learn how to look to the future rather than the past. These sessions helped me to understand why I was so upset all the time. I saw the counsellor six times. Although I felt able to discuss anything with her, without having to worry about anyone else's feelings, I didn't think it was helping me much. Looking back, though, it was not because the counsellor couldn't help me. Rather the opposite, I think. I now understand that she was helping me so much that she had actually begun to break down long held defences.

On a good day I believed everything was fine. I had found Mai and Tony, and I am happy with what I have learned. Nothing is wrong and I am the happiest girl in the world. Adoption is *not* an issue. Ignore any bad feelings so they can't hurt me and they will go away! But when I spent an hour with the counsellor, I found my ability to keep unwanted feelings at bay weakening, and I did not like losing control. I was the tough one, and I was not yet ready to unleash my emotions and admit that I did have problems with being adopted. This would have meant admitting that I was hurting, which would have forced me to examine why and feel the pain. I was also beginning to plan my wedding, and I was finding it increasingly difficult to deal with the day-to-day aspects of my life when my mind was in turmoil.

I did stop going after only a few sessions, but counselling or simply chatting with someone who was independent, during that short amount of time, managed to show me that I did not have to fear talking about my needs. I did not have to apologise for need-ing Mai in my life, if that was what I decided was for the best. The counsellor helped me to accept that my family was a constant in my life and they had loved me for so long that their love would not disappear if I decided to renew contact with Mai. I knew that, deep down, I just needed to say it out loud. She also made me realise that I had nothing to lose in moving forward with Mai. I was able to look at the worst that could happen and to take each challenge in small steps, to overcome any hurt in an adult way. Yes, if I tried to get to know Mai and it didn't work out, I would be hurt, and probably hurt badly, but it couldn't be worse than the state of limbo I seemed to be stuck in now, could it?

If the truth be known, I could not stop thinking of Mai and her gang up in Wicklow. Aidan and I married shortly afterwards, in

August 1999, and they were in my thoughts on that day. She knew the date and I wondered was she thinking of me. Another year passed in the flurry of getting used to being a wife and learning to share my life with my husband and face whatever life had in store for us. As any newly married couple might tell you, it was a time of great change and we learned this new way of life together. I also changed jobs to one nearer to home as Personnel Manager and threw myself into this new challenge. Yet always constant in my heart was the knowledge that my birth family still did not know about me, and this meant there was sadness in my life.

I had started to become comfortable talking about this sadness with Mum and Dad and was acutely aware of the void in my heart. There were still occasions when it had the ability to overwhelm me at the least expected times, doing the housework or tending to the garden, times when my mind would wander and settle on life in Wicklow and what it must be like. But we muddled through, and when Mum and Dad thought it was safe to bring up the subject of Wicklow, always aware of how sensitive a subject it was, we would sometimes talk about the possibility of renewing contact with Mai and how I might go about this. They knew, of course, that I could not be pushed into this decision – it had to come from me.

During those years I allowed myself to think about Mai and, in time, about what I wanted, but I did not allow myself to fully express the ensuing emotions. I could let myself feel them little by little, and if they brought too much hurt, then I shut them off and lost myself in my new job or a task at home, painting the kitchen or clearing out the shed. Matters came to a head when I lost my job in June 2002. I had been employed as Human Resource Manager for two years, and when the company was taken over this position was surplus to needs within the new management structure.

I have since been able to understand the effect this had on me and, in a way, how it made me look in the mirror and admit a few home truths about myself. After I lost my job I felt a complete failure. I understand now that it was not because I did not have the skills required by the new owners or that I was not a good enough manager. At the time, however, I believed that it was me personally who had been rejected. Not the job, but me. I was paralysed by this feeling. I had always needed to be perfect, to be the best at anything I attempted, to prove that I had a right to exist.

The unworthiness I felt after the loss of my job threw me into a depression, and yet, paradoxically, those weeks were the saving of me. While I had nothing else to do but sit at home and clean and bake, and think about me, my beliefs and, of course, Mai and Wicklow, I seemed unable to run away from how I felt any longer. My emotions took hold and overwhelmed me.

In March of that year, on my birthday, Aidan arrived home early one afternoon and gave me a violin, something I had always wanted to learn to play, yet I sat on the bed and cried. I laugh now, because the poor man thought he had purchased the wrong one and upset me in some way. We truly talked that afternoon. Even though I had been applying for jobs at every turn, it was proving very hard to find employment. But that afternoon we laughed, and we both knew that it was only a matter of time before something turned up and my luck changed. I simply had no choice but to accept my feelings, to really feel them and grieve for lost years, for silly dreams, and to accept reality – not only for my sake, but also for Aidan's. And I had to have the courage to look to the future and not be afraid of what it held for me. That day I decided there was to be no more running away from my past. I dried my eyes and looked in the mirror and a really lucky girl looked back at me. She was ashamed at the self-indulgent way she had been living and decided that this was the time to make changes. I had to take control of my life, not let it control me.

Aidan and I talked that afternoon of how we could best kick-start the relationship between Mai and me. Aidan is and always will be a firm believer in seizing the moment, despite the consequences. Before I had a chance to change my mind, Aidan had grabbed the phoned and called Mai. They spoke for nearly half an hour, while my nerves would not allow me to talk to her on the phone. I stood outside the door listening to the words I could catch and cried. What could I say to her? Sorry would have been the way to start, but there was time enough for that. One of the most difficult things for me, after nearly four years since the news first broke about them, was the knowledge that I had seven other birth brothers and sisters and they still did not know of my existence.

During the phone call, Aidan broached the subject of when Mai thought she might tell them. She always said that she certainly would tell them, but after so many years, five at this stage, I began to question whether this would ever happen. She spoke of waiting for the right time to tell the kids, and I had to do my best to remain patient. This was something Mai had to do when she was ready. I tried to understand that this was the right thing to do, that there could really be no other way, but it was difficult.

So we resumed contact this way and slowly we began to write letters and phone one another on and off. It was still hard for me to phone Mai, however, as the two youngest at that time, aged five and six, would have started to become aware of my calling the house and questions might have been asked. One day at home a number of years previously, and shortly after I had met Mai, she telephoned me and we chatted for a while. I could hear Lisa, my little sister, running around Mai's feet. Mai asked me if I wanted to say hello to her and I agreed, yet wasn't quite sure what to say. For Mai it might have seemed an easy thing to do, to talk to this little girl, but it was a conversation that broke my heart. I held it together as best I could and we said hello. Lisa asked me who I was and I told her I was a friend of Mummy's. She seemed happy with this explanation, and after a minute or two of small talk about school and what she was doing for the day, she got bored and handed me back to Mai.

I cried bitter tears and after only a minute or two had to say goodbye to Mai. I had found the time talking with Lisa just too hard. I wanted so much for Mai's sake to be able to accept her decision, because I knew she was waiting for the right time, but after that day I knew, without a doubt, that I had to get to know my birth brothers and sisters. It was no longer something that would be nice for me to do: it was a necessity. Mum has told me since, and my memory of this is hazy, that she stood outside the door while I hung up the phone and released tears that had been kept inside for far too long.

So, now that we were in contact once again, Mai telephoned me whenever she could when she was alone. I began to trust her, and even though we began to learn snippets about each other, the process was painfully slow. We both had been hurt after our mistakes the last time and were wary of each other. I am not a patient person, and I know Mai began to feel this impatience. I tried hard not to pressure her about telling the rest of her gang, but I guess I did, despite my best efforts. They began to play on my mind each day.

A few months passed and I imagine Mai and Tony went through a rough time. It must have taken them a lot of courage to tell the people they loved most about a child they gave up over twenty-seven years ago. As it turns out, they all knew something was worrying Mai terribly, but no one knew what it was. One of the girls actually thought that there was another baby on the way! But life had forced Mai and Tony's hand, because the decision to tell the children was made after a bad car accident that one of her younger sons, my 'little' brother, Tony Junior (J. R.), had been in. It was a miracle he managed to walk out of it alive, and in Mai's own words, she thought, if anything had happened to Tony Jnr without meeting me, she would never have forgiven herself.

I think the plan was to tell them all over Sunday lunch some afternoon. However, Mai told Breda (who was twenty-five at the time) first, and she took the news well. In Breda's words, 'If you had let me walk up the aisle without knowing about her, I would have killed you, Mam!' Within the week, each of the older children found out about me. A week after Breda was told about me, she sent me a letter and I replied. Her letter was filled with a sense of awe and humour – 'Hi, Claire, my name is Breda and I guess I'm your sister ... Howaya ... What are you like?' Just what the doctor ordered. This was a girl I knew I would like – a lot.

I was in the pub with Aidan a night or two after the children found out and I received a call from Breda. I couldn't answer the call. I didn't know what to say. I texted back and said as much. After some messages, a few more drinks and much encouragement from Aidan, I rang the number and had my first conversation with my birth sister from Wicklow. We were both very nervous but we laughed and, although we only spoke a few words, we promised to write. We exchanged a few letters, and after about two weeks I received a phone call from Joe (twenty-seven), Mary (eighteen), J. R. (twenty-three) and Eoin (fifteen). Kieran and Lisa were still too young to understand, so they were told I was a friend of Breda's from college.

Again my impatience got the better of me. Having waited for the best part of five years since I had first learned about them all, after only a few short weeks, a couple of texts and letters later, I had arranged for the five older kids, Joe, Breda, J. R., Mary and Eoin, their partners and a friend of the family to come to Cork for the October weekend. None of us had any idea really what to expect, and for the second time in my life I was scared out of my wits.

I have often thought since getting to know them that it was an amazing thing for them all to come down to Cork, to people they had never met before, and stay with us for a long weekend. I remember Joe, the eldest in Wicklow, calling me and telling me that it was really no big deal for them to stay in a Bed and Breakfast. I am so glad they stayed with us, however, as it was the wee hours of the morning, sitting around the kitchen table, that helped us all gel so well in those early days. I had asked that the kids only come down, without Mai and Tony, or Mum and Dad, as I was still nervous after our earlier mistakes, and I wanted to be as relaxed as possible in this new situation. Apart from a few phone calls and letters, Mai and I still had not seen one another since our first meeting and we still had much to talk about.

Here again was a group of people, my brothers and sisters, who were related to me by blood, yet I had no idea what they were like. I was about to entertain them and their girlfriends and boyfriends for three days and three nights, and we might not even like each other! I already had feelings for them, even though I had not met them. But I knew it was possible that there might never be any bond between us, despite my feelings. It has always been my greatest fear, to love someone and not have the feeling returned, to be rejected, as I had believed happened on 19 March 1974.

The days before were spent scrubbing every inch of the house, ironing sheets, cooking chilli con carne, cleaning skirting boards and God only knows what else. I was so anxious to make a good impression, I went to a tanning salon the day before they came and arrived home looking like a Satsuma!

All that remained to do was stock up on drink and hope for the best.

11

THE GANG

I will never forget the night before my birth brothers and sisters arrived. I think it was worse than meeting Mai and Tony. So much had gone wrong between Mai and I. What if the same thing happened again?

I didn't sleep at all that Thursday night. I had to do this alone. No matter how much Aidan wanted to protect me from worries and concerns, I was the person they had come to meet. This was the culmination of years of worry, wonder and terror at what might happen if ever we were to meet. The house was clean and ready by Friday lunchtime. I had been sick twice by then. Those afternoon hours were the longest of my life. I listened to music, my thoughts running riot. (Even Bob Dylan and Christy did not help!)

I was determined to do this on my own, and Mum, Dad and Mary were going to pop in on Bank Holiday Monday for a few hours and meet them all, whatever the outcome after the weekend. Until then, I was going solo. I don't think I fully appreciated how difficult it was for the gang to arrive into our home, also not knowing what to expect, willing to meet me and just let it happen, to see what sort of a person this 'sister' of theirs was. It took a lot of courage. Still, they had each other, and meeting them all at once was daunting, but it was the way I had arranged it.

I have asked myself would it have been better to meet them one by one, and it might have been easier for me, but then stories might have passed between them about how each meeting went, and opinions might have been formed by those who hadn't met me. I also don't think we would have been really ourselves under those circumstances. Mind you, I was so nervous that weekend that they only saw glimpses of the real Claire Cashin, and I am only now beginning to be truly myself in their company. However, I don't think any of us were quite prepared for how that first night and, in fact, the whole weekend went.

We received a phone call from Joe and Breda about nine on Friday night and they took directions from Aidan to meet him at the Silversprings Hotel, so he could guide them to our home. He gave me a hug and told me he would be back in a short time. As he said himself since, the weekend could have been one of two things: a roaring success or a complete disaster. Well, he was right! It was a cold night, and from the moment Aidan left me, I took my cigarettes outside the door and stood there, smoking one after another. Thoughts, worries and fears rushed through my brain so quickly that I could not catch one thought. My palms were wet, my stomach in knots and my one concern was, 'Don't cry, don't cry, be nice and relaxed, don't exert any pressure.' I thought of my family in Cork and of Mai and Tony, knowing they must also be nervous about what was ahead and not being able to be a part of it, worrying for us all and wondering.

Still, as before, this was something that needed to be done alone, without having to be concerned about anyone other than those present. I worried about how to greet these people: do I hug them; do I offer a handshake; do I simply say hello? Some of the things that passed through my mind were ridiculous – did I put out the new towels; did I spray air freshener; were the dogs washed? I was so worried about what type of people they were and what they would think. As it turned out, all my worries about the initial meeting were unfounded; they simply took the situation in hand and made it very easy for me. I can never do all of these people justice, for each and every one of them is amazing, I can only give you glimpses of the people they are and what they mean to me.

The cars arrived and turned in the drive. I popped a tic tac in my mouth and waited for them to park. Breda was first out of the car. She came towards me with confidence and immediately gave me a hug that said everything's going to be OK. Again I thought, 'Don't cry, don't cry!' Joe was next and gave me a kiss on the cheek. I was worried about meeting Joe – being the eldest, I wondered how he would react to me. I need not have worried: as one of the most compassionate, honest and caring men I have ever met, he is still teaching me valuable lessons. Mary and Eoin said hello warmly and they went into the kitchen. Sue and Jonathon, Joe and Breda's partners, stayed in the background and then came in. Tony Junior (JR) and Paul, a friend of Tony's, were due to arrive the following day.

When I came into the kitchen and saw all these faces looking up at me, I was so afraid I could have been sick right there in front of them – was I mad? I simply opened the fridge, told them to help themselves to the beer, food or whatever they would need for the weekend. They were to make themselves feel at home. Within five minutes they all had a drink, and I sat down. It was obviously a very weird situation to be in, but we all decided to just have a laugh and to see what happened. I didn't cry when they arrived and was very proud of myself for holding it together – at least until the wee hours of that night.

I sat and listened to the craic and the stories about their growing-up years, and I sorted them out with beds for the night. I had cooked a shepherd's pie, and I'm not usually a bad cook. That shepherd's pie, though, was a disaster. The potato was soggy but, bless them, they ate without complaint and, like myself, had a few drinks. Aidan took out the guitar and the bodhrán and we soon had a sing-song. Everyone was on form and a rip-roaring session went on into the small hours. This was one of the first things I learned about them, that they love music, and thank God for that. I think we all quickly realised that, even though we didn't know each other well yet, we seemed to have certain things in common. Maybe the weekend would not be a disaster after all.

That first night was great fun and we seemed to get on very well. As the drink flowed and the tongues loosened, I would catch one of them looking at some physical trait of mine or vice versa. Joe pointed out I had Tony Senior's (my birth dad's) hands, for example. Then something else would be noted and we would all laugh at one another. Breda and Mai had made a photo album of them all over the years and we laughed at similarities between us. It was a strange and wonderful night. I am so glad that we had the whole weekend, as we had only just started and there was still no mention of the whole issue of my adoption.

The hours flew and, before I knew it, it was 4 a.m. and Joe, Breda, Mary, Eoin and myself remained around the table. I can't quite remember how this conversation started, maybe because of the copious amount of cocktails I had made, but perhaps there had been a small lull.

We began to talk of me as their adopted 'sister'. What followed was one of the most special moments of the weekend and showed me that the whole issue of being adopted was not taboo – it was nothing to worry about. The words that Joe spoke took a lot of courage, and I have never discussed them with him since. As a group of people, and for Joe especially, the subject of adoption and what happened in the past did not seem as important as building our relationships for the future. That said, I don't think he under-stood what he did for me that night. He made things very simple and I am grateful from the bottom of my heart.

He said that he knew the same blood ran through our veins, but that I was not a sister yet, in the sense that Breda, Mary and

Lisa were. He grew up with them, he said, and his love and care for them came from many years of growing up together. He spoke the truth and I replied, 'Of course.' That *was* the reality of the situation. The words came to me inside again, 'Don't cry, don't cry.' This time, though, the tears came, no matter how hard I tried to stop them. They slipped out quietly, and I think I made an excuse to go to the bathroom.

I needed to get outside for fresh air. I wasn't upset at what Joe had said, as such, because it was the truth and I knew that already. But his words cleared the air, they brought to the fore what needed to be said and I felt such a release and a weight go from my shoulders. Joe said the words straight out, showing me that although I was adopted this was not a taboo for them, but that we would look to the future and see what happened. He did not seem worried, as I was, and his honesty was a breath of fresh air.

At that moment, I knew I would love them all, whether they liked it or not, and I hoped they would become a part of my life. I cried because someone had spoken the truth openly and for the first time, I don't know why, I felt it was OK to cry for what could have been. He had spoken to me with honesty, without worrying about hurting my feelings, without worrying about saying the *correct* thing. I felt I could count on him from here on out to be this honest about anything. I realised that I couldn't change the years gone by and it was time to accept this and move on.

I started to grieve, at that moment, for all the years of not knowing and not understanding. I began to understand why my heart felt heavy and that it was all right to feel this way. Joe came out to me and, God bless him, apologised for saying what he had and for hurting me. He hugged me tight, and while I tried to explain that what he'd said had not hurt my feelings, I didn't have the words to express it. We spoke some more, just he and I, smoked a cigarette and put the world to rights. It was time for bed.

There are so many important memories of that weekend that simply made me realise that I might have a future with these people.

Aidan had a rally the next day and the lads joined him to watch one of their great passions in life. I phoned Mum and Dad and Rachael and cried with joy at how easy it had been. I also had the chance to spend some time with Breda and Mary on my own. I learned some things about their childhoods and we shared some information. I was nervous being on my own with them at first and wasn't sure what to say, but it seemed natural just to be myself and see what happened. I had yet to meet Tony Jnr (J.R.) and, even though we had all hit it off so far, I worried about this next member of the family to arrive.

It was a nice day. Breda told me I looked lovely, that what I was wearing looked great on me – it's funny the things you remember! J. R. arrived later that afternoon with Paul, his friend, and I went to meet them with Breda and Mary. His Landcruiser pulled up and out hopped a male Claire! My God, we looked so alike. I kissed him on the cheek and we went and did some shopping and got back to the house. That night, we all shared stories of the previous night. It was the first time a story was told that I was part of, part of them! Then we went up to the local pub and attempted another sing-song, with not as much success as the night before.

We sat and talked, and J. R. and I seemed to click straight away. I remember later that night, or early the next morning rather, Joe, Breda, J. R. and I were sitting at the table, and I can't remember exactly what the context of the conversation was but it concerned the fact that I was adopted and what the future held for us as a group. It was a little close to the bone for me, and I didn't say much. I did not want to discuss what the future held for us because it terrified me that I would not be part of it.

J. R. looked at me and pointed out that we both had moles on our faces, practically in the same spot, something I had noticed. I smiled and, without realising it, had wrapped my hands into a tight fist. J. R. saw my hands, clutched tight in an effort to keep my emotions at bay. He asked me to give him my hand and I just couldn't. I wanted to let my guard down, but I was so afraid of feeling something for them all and of being hurt. He grabbed my hand and pulled me to him and hugged me, told me I was terrible at hugging and that I needed lessons! I broke my heart laughing and hugged him back, with all my strength. Another one of the gang had broken down a piece of the wall I had spent twenty-eight years building up around myself.

The next day was spent relaxing, on the Playstation or catching up on sleep and sharing bits of information about one another. We went into Cork that night and met up with some friends. I would have loved my sister Mary to join us that night, but it was difficult for her and she wasn't up to meeting us. She would have enjoyed the craic. Everyone was flabbergasted at how much we all looked like each other. We were all relaxed enough with each other and started to joke and take the mickey. It was a fun night. We went on to a late bar and I attempted to arm wrestle both J. R. and Joe, something I had done with Dad time and time again. I will *never* try that again – my arm took days to recover and, needless to say, they beat me time and time again. God loves a trier. When we arrived home that night everyone went to bed except J. R. and myself, and at about 5 a.m. we decided to go for a drive.

We ended up at the Dock beach in Kinsale. The sea was wild, reflecting the emotions running riot inside me. I will always remember the drive down to Kinsale, about an hour from our home. J. R. and I joked and laughed as if we had known one another for many years. When we reached the beach, we sat and talked and watched the sun come up. We discussed being adopted and my life in Cork for the previous twenty-eight years and we shared stories about our years growing up, past loves, future plans and about this first meeting and what could happen from here.

I can't explain why but we clicked immediately. From the moment we met I felt comfortable with him and able to share anything with him. Perhaps it's because we are both very passionate people, and when we start something we commit to it. It's all or nothing, something that was to become a deciding factor in our relationship as time progressed.

It was a special morning. I was aware that Mum and Dad and Mary were arriving for lunch but not that worried about the time. So we walked a while and chatted some more. At 11 a.m. Tony received a phone call asking where we were and saying we needed to come back. I really had no idea what the rush was, so we took our time and arrived back for about midday. Another hurdle awaited me – one that I was completely unprepared for.

As a surprise, Mai and Tony had stayed in a Bed and Breakfast in Fermoy and had arranged to arrive at our house on Monday with Kieran and Lisa, the same day my own family were due to arrive. I know Mai and Tony and the gang had arranged the surprise in an effort to include everyone and thought I would be delighted. It's not that I didn't want to see them, and if my family were not due to arrive, then it would have been different. The surprise was well intentioned – that is the important thing.

I walked into the house full of the joys and Aidan told me who was on the way. I did not take the news well. The house was a mess; Mum and Dad could not be contacted to let them know what was ahead. It didn't help that I had been up all night and was a wreck. After a few sleepless nights, I become decidedly waspish! A very emotional moment was about to take place: both my families, and *especially* both sets of parents, were about to meet for the first time, and this was not the way I had envisioned it. I needed to build up to things; I needed to prepare. Mai and I had not seen each other since things had begun to turn sour between us and this terrified me.

My family had prepared themselves to meet the children and spend some time getting to know them. The meeting of Mai and Tony and Colum and Eileen was a big deal for me. It was, in fact, the biggest moment in the whole search and reunion saga – these four people would have to meet eventually, but how would they all get on? After I heard the news, I went down to the bedroom and slammed the door. I know I made them all feel very uncomfortable that day, but I was as angry as hell. I had not spoken much to Mai since we had fallen out, and a lot needed to be said, on our own. That was something that still terrified me, never mind worrying about Mum and Dad and how this would make them feel. Jonathon, Sue and Paul (the girlfriends and boyfriends) disappeared, as it was obvious things might get a little heated. The girls grabbed the Hoover and cleaned the bathroom and so on while I tried to make myself look a little less like someone who had been out all night.

I came out of my room and tried to avoid talking to any of them. I attempted to keep my anger and fear about meeting Mai to myself, but Joe cornered me and made me sit down at the kitchen table. I just sat and cried and tried to explain what I was feeling, how nervous I was of meeting Mai again and how worried I was about Mum and Dad. I felt sick, but he hugged me and told me it would be fine.

Shortly afterwards, Mai and Tony arrived with the two little ones, Kieran and Lisa, who were six and seven then. Someone had obviously telephoned Mai, and she said again they would only stay for a cup of tea and then be on their way again. I tried to hide my surprise and I gave her a hug, but a lot still needed to be said between us. I reassured her that, of course, they were going nowhere: they would stay for something to eat and that was that.

She was uncomfortable, that was obvious, and partly my fault as the gang had already explained my reaction to the news of their arrival, but I did my best to hide how I felt about their visit and tried to make the best of the situation.

They had arrived about half an hour before Mum, Dad and Mary, and all the while I was trying to get in contact with them about Mai and Tony but with no success.

Parts of that day were so surreal. All Lisa wanted was to sit with the grown ups and this new 'friend' of Breda's, while Kieran wanted to know when the next chocolate bar was coming and how to change the 'bloody view on the Playstation'. While I did my best to be calm and make tea and make Mai and Tony feel welcome in our home, I was unsure what to say. So much needed to be sorted out; so much anger had passed between us over the years. We made the best of the situation. I know the surprise of their visit was intended to make me happy, to be a nice end to a great weekend. But, and I say this not with the intention of hurting Mai and Tony, it hurt a little that they had not considered how difficult the meeting might be for Mum and Dad or the way in which I had wanted the weekend to go.

I felt completely helpless and had no control over the way the afternoon went. The doorbell went and Mum and Dad had arrived. I stepped outside and told them what had happened. Dad hugged me and Mum just said, 'All right, it's OK – let's go inside, calm down and take it easy.' They laughed and told me to relax. They put smiles on their faces and walked in and made it all right for me. Mary and Michael, her boyfriend, arrived shortly afterwards, and we sat in the kitchen while most of the gang stayed in the TV room.

There were tears and hugs from Mai and Eileen, Colum and Tony and Mary and Michael. My poor sister was completely stressed out and was trying so hard to hide it, but it was a tough day for her. Lisa hovered, taking everything in, and asked me why her mum was crying. I told her that there was a lot of smoke in the room and her eyes were watering. She went over to the patio door and opened it wide, freezing us all. It was funny, yet sad at the same time. Of course, she had no idea what was happening. I made tea and kept busy and, even though exhausted, tried to be the hostess. After a short while, Joe and Breda came in and joined us, and I appreciated so much their not only wanting to support Mai and Tony, but also making the effort to get to know my family.

We had a bite to eat. Pictures were taken of the two families together and the afternoon passed without event. At long last, everyone had met and I could accept that what I had expected to be an ordeal was at long last over. After seven years, this was the moment I had hoped for, and it was worth every tear and worry.

Late afternoon, everyone decided to make a move, and Mum, Dad and Mary were the first to leave. With a combination of thanks for what had transpired, relief after a weekend of roller-coaster emotions and pure exhaustion, I started to cry and Tony Snr and Dad were next to me. Tony made a move to give me a hug, but it was only natural for me to turn to Dad for a hug and reassurances that everything was all right. It made me sad and again highlighted that, even though these were the people who had brought me into the world, it was Colum and Eileen who I knew as Mum and Dad and loved as such. It was clear to me that we had a long, long way to go yet.

It was no-one's fault but I was feeling like piggy in the middle. I loved Mum and Dad and Mary and I worried about them thinking I felt any different towards them. I worried about not exerting pressure on the gang, to not make them feel obliged to feel anything towards a stranger. I worried about hurting Mai and Tony and how they would feel seeing me with Mum and Dad and turning to them for support when upset. I worried about getting to know Mai and having to talk about what happened in the past few years and how to make amends. And I worried about what was going to happen now and if the gang from Wicklow still wanted to continue to get to know me. I worried myself sick, I suppose.

It was an amazing weekend. I think God must believe I'm not such a bad person to pull this all together for me and I am thankful for it. I had faced some of my greatest fears during that weekend and came out the other side.

I was now able to look forward with and more importantly, back with a sense of perspective. I needed to forgive and to accept what could not now be changed. Only then could I move on with my life instead of wishing 'if only ...'

12

IT SUDDENLY
DAWNED ON ME

Mum and Dad told me for the first time recently, about when I seemed to realise that somewhere out there I actually had another mummy. I was aged nine and had asked them to visit St Patrick's Guild in Dublin for my birthday to see the babies there. I don't know if I fully appreciated where exactly I was at that age or what had happened here. I just knew this was where Mum and Dad and Mary had collected me and from where I was brought to Cork. On the way home in the car, I turned to Mum and Dad and said, 'So, I have another mummy?'

They have told me I was a little thoughtful on the way home. This may have been the point in my life when I was able to grasp the meaning of adoption, in terms other than not growing in Mummy's tummy. This realisation and every hurt and misunderstanding that had settled during the intervening years came to a shuddering halt the moment my siblings from Wicklow left on that bank holiday Monday. If I can be certain of nothing else in my life, I am sure that was the moment, for the first time in my life, that I accepted I was adopted and that I had to let go of the past and everything that haunted me. Easier said than done, but I accepted the possibility of a different life and what that might have been like if circumstances had been different. Not better, nor worse, just *different*.

I had lived my life up until then acknowledging the fact that I was adopted, and certainly loved by my family, yet not wishing to think about that other mum and the reason she gave me away. This would have opened the floodgates to all my fears and worries and shaken what little self-belief I had. To learn of a birth mother and father and that other children existed was also something, up until that evening, I had not wished to think about much. I let myself believe that I wanted nothing more than for us all to meet each other, yet I had still pushed one question to the dark recesses of my mind: 'What if things had been different?' This question may be hard to understand and it might read like I'm comparing the two worlds. Nothing could be further from the truth, for my family in Cork are just that, my mum, dad and sister.

Always present, however, was the knowledge that my bloodline came from somewhere else. After meeting the Wicklow gang, it was clear that not only did we share a bloodline, but also we had a connection of sorts. I don't know if I believe that blood is thicker than water, but this tie, and the security and relief this connection can provide, was a balm that soothed many preconceived notions I had, specifically concerning my self-esteem and worthiness to be loved.

That weekend in October 2002 was nothing like I had expected, despite trying hard not to expect anything at all. I had not prepared myself for how well we would all get on, even click, with each other. You sometimes meet people you are lucky enough to share a sense of humour with, or a love of music, or a similar outlook on life, and you continue to get to know these people as friends. I had not prepared myself for how much we already seemed to know one another, despite being strangers, for as the weekend progressed we began to notice expressions, a hand movement, a look, that we all shared. Physically, I am like many of them – mainly the boys. I was not blessed with the girls' slim hips!

Years ago I believed every part of your personality was taught by and learned from those closest to you, your family. Much of what I have learned, how to treat others, to help where I can, my morals and beliefs and the type of person I hope to be, has come from the example I was set at home. But I cannot escape the fact that there are many aspects of who I am that I now believe to be genetic. When united with other family members I have learned that with this bond of blood comes an inescapable return to my roots.

It is still quite amazing to me that, even though none of the gang had ever met me before, every one of them came down to Cork, to my home with Aidan, and were willing enough to share three whole days and nights with me. It could easily have been a complete disaster. They're a very open and trusting bunch and have accepted me wholeheartedly into their family unit, as one of their own, in some ways. That weekend they taught me that I had to let go a little of the hurt they could see in me. I needed to learn to trust them. I needed to leave the past behind. They wanted to get to know me from here on out.

People who meet under normal circumstances generally do not share this intensity of feeling or bond from the outset. We all shared some very intimate moments during that weekend and at the end, when they walked out the door, I was terrified that I would not be accepted by them. I was already in too deep and had feelings for them. Despite my innate need to protect myself, my awareness that I shouldn't get too attached, they had already, after only a few days, worn down my defences and become part of my life.

I can say with my hand on my heart that this was the most difficult time of my search – not knowing what would happen. It's one thing to get caught up in the craic of a great weekend, and another to look at it in the cold light of day and think about what it meant for the future. After everyone left that bank holiday Monday, I sat on the hall floor and let my emotions take hold. I cried for a long time that night, tears of happiness but moreover tears of sorrow at what might have been had a different decision been made. That's not an accusation, for it was because of her love for me that Mai did what she thought was best. Nor is it a wish to have been born part of their family, for how could I now consider giving up the love of my family here in Cork?

It was merely sorrow at having seen both sides and allowing myself to grieve, to let go of any anger I might have felt and the belief I was given away because I was not loved. I cried for close to a week, mostly on my own, and the tears I shed washed away much of the hurt and sorrow I had denied. I grieved for a long time for the life I had lost in Wicklow, for the steps I now had to take to forge a closer relationship with this new group of people and with Mai and Tony. It was clear to me that I had to build bridges with my birth mother, and all this without forgetting about how much I loved them all in Cork.

I shared many of these feelings of sorrow with Mum and Dad and yet felt very alone at times, unable to understand my own feelings. I couldn't put them into words for others to understand. I missed them all in Wicklow already and spent many hours mulling over the events and memories of the Bank Holiday weekend, using them as blocks to build upon. Again wise words came from Mum and Dad to take my time and not to rush into anything. They must have been worried, to see their daughter so confused and in danger of being hurt by people they really didn't know very well.

Again, however, I didn't listen, and within two weeks I paid my first visit to Wicklow. This was a difficult time for Mai and Tony. They had taken the very courageous step of telling their immediate family about me, but still their brothers and sisters and relatives had to be told. Mai was simply not ready, and I knew that when the time was right for her she would tell them. I had waited too many years to just wait and see and was very excited about meeting the gang on their home ground. I found my way from Dublin with the help of a map. It wasn't too difficult to find. I stayed incognito in a Bed and Breakfast booked by one of my sisters – and paid for, I might add: they spoil me rotten still! I was terribly nervous, and if I could do it all over again, I probably would have waited a little longer and tried to get to know them better first.

However, I met Breda in the hotel where she worked and waited until she finished. I sat there bursting with excitement, looking at the place where my brothers and sisters had grown up, yet in the eyes of the locals I was just another tourist. Before long the whole gang had arrived, determined to show me a good time. One of the locals there that night had noticed the physical similarities between us and asked what the connection was. I wanted to shout and scream, 'I'm their sister – thank you so much for noticing,' yet for the sake of Mai, Tony and the family I replied, 'Oh yeah, I think there might be some connection there going back a few years, a distant relative maybe.' We had great craic that night and saw in the dawn.

After breakfast the next day, I called Mai and Tony and arranged to call up to their house on my own. In Kieran and Lisa's minds I was still just a friend of Breda's from college. It was very emotional driving up to their home and seeing them in their own surroundings. At this stage, I think I knew the kids better than Mai and Tony – we had certainly spent more time together and had the chance to find out about one another. I was very nervous that day and, with hindsight, I should have waited a while before visiting. Tony's sister was very sick at this time, and I think, with everything going on, the timing wasn't quite right. We drank coffee and chatted and shared some small pieces of information about my years growing up and their own experiences, yet we still had to talk about the past and the mistakes we had made. It was easier to chat about everyday matters and stories of growing up and share a laugh than talk about the hurt we both felt. I stayed there that night.

The following day, J. R. brought myself, Kieran and Lisa up to his farm and, boy, was I ever a city girl! (The gang have since bought me wellies!) It was wet and muddy weather and we went to feed the cows. Of course, I was determined to help, to show how much of an animal lover I am. But to reach the cows at the other side, we had to cross a field. Kieran and Lisa ran across the grass, dodging cow pats effortlessly as if floating across the muddy field. I made my mind up: I was damned if I was going to look an eejit in front of them. Things didn't go quite to plan.

They were trying to slow down without making me feel silly, and I tried to speed up so as not to look stupid. I had never been within fifty feet of a cow before in my life. The going was tough and the mud was thick and it was easy to get bogged down. We managed eventually to get the bales of hay into the cows and began to make our way back. J. R. got back in his tractor well before I managed to reach the bank. Kieran and Lisa also reached the ditch long before I managed to struggle back to them, so all three were standing on the ditch laughing at my painful progress through the mud. It certainly didn't help that I was not used to walking in wellies.

Kieran, all of six years of age, jumped down to help me back up, when all of a sudden both my wellington boots became entrenched in a large puddle of mud. I tried valiantly to free myself by loosening one of my legs, but the more I struggled the more I seemed to sink. Before I knew it, I was knee deep. I gave one last wriggle to try and free myself and, without any warning, I completely lost my balance and ended up sitting in the biggest cow pat I have ever seen! My bottom was well and truly stuck, my legs completely useless and my hands grappled for any hold. Kieran roared laughing and all I could see ahead of me were J. R. and Lisa doubled over in stitches. All I could do was laugh until all three pulled me out of my predicament. My escapades were enjoyed by all.

Later that day, having recovered from my adventure with the cows, Kieran, Lisa and myself were messing about in some pools of mud, chatting, while J. R. was fixing a tractor. Kieran, one of the sharpest kids I have ever met, looked up at me and started to ask me some questions that I was not at all prepared for. 'What school did you go to?' he asked. 'Ah, you wouldn't know it,' I answered. 'What college did you go to?' and I answered, 'A college in Shannon.' Wrong answer! Without even waiting to breathe, he pounced and stated that Breda, his sister, went to Carlow Institute of Technology and that if I was a college friend, then how come we didn't go to the same college? I said that we'd met through mutual friends. He asked me what age I was. I told him twenty-eight. (Breda was twenty-five at this time). He looked at me once more, stated that all his friends were the same age as him and stalked off. Lisa was also hanging on every word.

I knew the plan was unstuck and explained to Mai and Tony about our little conversation. They were faced with what to do, and if the little ones were told then the news would be out. Tony decided to concoct the story that, in fact, I was their sister, but that Mai and I had fallen out years before and so had lost contact with one another. While this would certainly let them know I was their sister, I did not want them thinking I did not care enough about them to get in contact over the years, so Mai told them the truth of the matter as best she could and explained what adoption meant. They just accepted it as something that had happened and concentrated on getting to know me from there on out.

Mai and Tony then decided to break the news to one and all – brothers, sisters, aunts, uncles. Before long, everyone knew. I spent three days with them all and was overwhelmed at the welcome they gave me. Leaving them after my visit was very hard. We were a couple of hundred miles apart and I wanted so much to stay and learn as much as I could. I was hungry for information about their lives. I also wanted to ask them if I would become a part of their lives forever, if I would indeed become someone important to them. But of course, it was early days.

That first time I left Wicklow I felt a wrench and was terribly weepy when I got home to Aidan. Two weeks later we both visited them and stayed with Mai and Tony. It was strange to be sleeping under the roof where you might have grown up if things had been different, and I lay awake for a number of nights wondering and trying to piece things together in my mind. But there was another visit a few weeks later that had a bearing on the way things were to go.

We had arranged to visit before Christmas, as I was going to spend the holiday with Mum and Dad and the family in Cork, as I have done every year. I had made two of Mai's favourite desserts and was looking forward to sitting down and enjoying a slice over a cup of tea and having a chat. J. R. met us and showed us the way. My sense of direction is for the birds. When we arrived, I was told that all of Mai and Tony's brothers and sisters and their respective wives and husbands had been gathered to welcome me and say hello.

When I learned outside the door what the plan was, my palms became sweaty and I was very nervous. I was about to walk into a room of nearly twenty people, all of whom were related to me but none of whom I had met before. I didn't know how to react to this, though I know it was well intentioned and came from the heart. They were all so lovely and warm towards me. It must have been interesting for them to see similarities to the rest of the gang, but when you're the object of those eyes, it was daunting. I felt a little odd that night.

It was so thoughtful of Mai and Tony to arrange a welcome like this, to show me I was part of the family, to be excited about me. But everything was just happening so quickly. I still really didn't know Mai and Tony or the kids and here I was meeting the extended family. I had become comfortable with the slow passing of time over the previous six years, but now that everyone knew about me, we were going at a great speed.

I found that night difficult, and after only a short few hours I asked Mai would it be all right to pop down to the pub to join the others. It must have seemed terribly rude of me, but I just couldn't cope with everyone. I was just keeping my head above water after meeting the gang, and with Kieran and Lisa being told – it was too soon to get to know what it means to be a part of such a large family group.

I left that weekend having been told by Mai and Tony that they loved me, and I was probably wrong, but I thought they expected that love back immediately. It wasn't that I wanted to withhold my love to punish them, but a love like that takes time. With Eileen, Mary and Colum, it had taken twenty-eight years.

I also was very aware of Mum, Dad and Mary at home and how worried they were about me, so I needed to get home and include them. I know Mary was taking the news of my visits very hard and looked on them as a threat to our own relationship. I did my best to talk to her about them and to include her, telling her of our antics when I visited them, but information of this kind was too much for her, so we did not discuss it really. I purchased 'special sister' books and cards every now and again, and Mum and Dad constantly asked me to be considerate and thoughtful and under-standing of her, which of course I tried to be. I could feel Mary's pain, and while I tried to understand it, it made me feel guilty for needing this new family in my life – they were the final piece of the puzzle falling into place for me.

I did my best during the weeks and months that followed and tried to find a way for both parts of my life, in Cork and Wicklow, to integrate. I realised that things were going very quickly with the gang in Wicklow, yet at home in Cork, things crawled along while we all tried to accept this change in our lives.

I felt torn in two, caught between the two lives. I was very confused and was about to experience another wave of emotions that were not easy to understand. I could not figure out how to put things in perspective and make everything all right.

I needed to regain a sense of direction and an element of control. Yet again, I needed to make some decisions.

13

MAKING A MESS OF THINGS

After that weekend I spent in Wicklow, I began to feel under pressure. Mai and Tony expressed their feelings for me and were very affectionate and welcoming. They showed me that they now considered me part of their family. I was over the moon to finally know them all, and after the huge amount of courage it took to tell their family about me, I now had the chance to build relationships with everyone. I am grateful to Mai and Tony for allowing me to be part of their family so early on, but in hindsight, things just happened far too quickly for me.

Mai had begun to talk to me openly about why I was given up for adoption and how sorry she was, how guilty she felt and how she would change things if she could. I think it was a chance for her to unburden herself of years of trauma and guilt. I was glad we were now speaking openly, but being the person she confided in was difficult and at times I was at a loss as to how I could help her. I began to believe that they wanted their daughter back. I was wrong, but it was a fear I had at that time.

I began to share my feelings with Mum and Dad and asked for their help, for they knew how important this new family was in helping me to heal old wounds, yet they also understood my fears. Shortly afterwards, a friend of my Mum's who had counselling experience in the area of adoption provided great words of comfort for me, and I suppose for my Mum. She told Mum that from here on out any decision had to be on my terms, that this was just the way it had to be and that everyone who really loved and cared for me would understand. She said that anything I was feeling was normal and to take things one step at a time instead of running before I could walk.

But as per usual, I broke into a sprint. I have never been good at expressing my feelings on a one-to-one basis, something that the gang in Wicklow are very good at. So, in an effort to try and explain how I was feeling before I ran away frightened, I decided to write a letter to all the older kids.

I told them I had to slow things down and back off. I tried my very best to explain honestly how I was feeling and how grateful I was to them for welcoming me into their family. I just did not know what to do about the pressure I was feeling. I had a family in Cork who were affected by my decision to search, and possibly a little threatened by it. And I wasn't sure that I could give the family in Wicklow what I thought they wanted of me. I tried to set some boundaries, explaining that I was simply very confused. I was *not* saying thanks but no thanks, merely asking them to stick with me and try and understand how afraid I was. I just needed to work things out.

In the letter I wrote about how hard it was for me to open up and be honest with my feelings, but that I would do my best. Perhaps I was overly honest. I tried to make them understand that they meant the world to me, but for a while I would have to back off and slow things down. I should have left it at that, but I went on to say that I was stopping all contact for the moment and didn't know when I would be in touch again.

I also wrote how hard I was finding it to deal with Mai's emotions and the guilt that she obviously felt, and that I wondered if it would help her to talk with a counsellor. This was like a red rag to a bull for many of them, especially Mai. She, I learned afterwards, took offence at this and seemed reluctant to admit that she was having difficulties with any aspect of our contact or the impact my adoption had had on her life. Some of the kids then took great offence at the suggestion that I might know their mother better than they did.

I don't think I explained myself very well in that letter, and I don't think some of them really understood what I was trying to say. I have learned that one of the most difficult things to do is put yourself in someone else's shoes and try to understand what they are going through. I failed miserably at that, and instead of talking about it, I wrote it down. I guess I'm not as good at writing letters as I thought I was.

I sent the letter to the five eldest children and tried to convey that every word was written with love for them all, despite my confusion. Most of them read it again and again and understood as best they could and cared for me enough to give me the space I needed. I include myself in this when I say that 'we' are all a hot-headed bunch.

I think we learned quite a bit about each other during the next few months. I hurt some of them quite badly with that letter and perhaps did more harm than good. I have damaged some of our relationships because of it. That letter was true to my feelings and although I am truly sorry some of it wasn't worded better, it was sent for the right reasons. I am only human and I make mistakes. I know I hurt Mai a lot with the letter. We have since talked about it, and I tried to explain that I referred to her and how hurt I believed she was because I care for her – there was no ulterior motive. I was just worried about her.

I think some of the gang believed that after all they had done for me, welcomed me, made me feel a part of them, to write a letter like that was throwing it back in their faces. Looking at the letter now, I can understand that. Their conviction that knew their mother better than I did could be right. All I know is, back then *I* was the person she confided in about her pain after my adoption, and I felt her pain so I knew to some extent what she was going through.

One of the kids accused me of trying to hurt Mai, to take revenge for being given up for adoption in the first place. I had many conversations with them afterwards, trying to make them understand that I was thankful for the chance Mai and Tony had given me in life. I tried to reassure them that I would not intentionally hurt any of them. How could I? I had spent the last eight years of my life dreaming about being a part of this family.

It was a tough time for me and, I guess, for them also. I was confused and I know I caused some of them to feel confused too. I regret wording things the way I did, but I have no regrets about trying to reach out to them through this letter, trying desperately to describe my innermost feelings. It took some courage to open myself up like that, and it gave me some time to try to understand my feelings and put things in perspective. I had built protective walls around myself, giving in to emotions only on my own terms. I began to feel love for these people, the strength of which shocked and terrified me. The reality is I just bolted, afraid of being hurt. But again, shortly afterwards, life with its twists and turns took control of our relationship.

A few months passed and, despite a few letters and texts, I spent this time thinking about what I wanted, just me. Some of the time I reverted to cutting my losses before I got hurt, afraid of being rejected by the gang. We all seemed to get on very well and I knew deep in my heart that I considered them to be brothers and sisters, yet I had no idea what kind of relationship they wanted. I knew I wanted them to feel love for me, but that was their call. I could not force them to feel anything for me. They would have to figure out for themselves what sort of relationship they wanted to build with me. I saw glimpses of how they felt, but I needed reassurances. It takes so long to build relationships, and one as delicate as this can be damaged easily.

I was at work one afternoon in July 2003 when I received a call from Joe, the eldest in Wicklow. I had not heard from any of them in months and they had respected my need to be on my own for all that time. Joe had called to tell me that Eoin, my sixteen-year-old brother, had been in a motorbike accident a few days ago and that they were unsure of how things would go. It was serious and some damage had been done to his brain. He was in intensive care in Beaumont Hospital in Dublin and Joe thought that I would want to know. I am glad he knew me well enough to realise that, although I needed some time to think, I would not hesitate to be with them at a time like this. I left work and went home to Mum and Dad, terrified at what might happen. I rang the hospital and told them I was his sister from Cork and enquired about his condition. Information was sketchy and they were unwilling to give a prognosis regarding his recovery. He was still unconscious after three days.

I made arrangements to take the early train to Dublin the next day, and Mum and Dad wanted to come with me, not only because I was upset, but also to offer any assistance they could to Mai and Tony. We arrived in Dublin early the next morning and went straight to the hospital. We met Mai and the rest of the gang there, and I wanted to see Eoin straight away. Mai came with me and my heart was in my mouth going into that room. I really was not prepared for seeing him like that, unconscious, machines breathing for him, with wires and monitors coming from everywhere, including his brain. His words from that first October weekend we met kept running through my head: 'Of course you're my sister.' After only nine months of knowing him, the fun and loving character that he is, I could not bear to have him taken 'from me'. We were united as those who shared a love for Eoin, and everything else was forgotten for the time being. Mum sat with him for a short while and tried to offer hope to Mai.

It was the first time I had seen them all in months, and most of them welcomed me with hugs and warm words as if nothing had passed between us. Two of my sisters were heavily pregnant at the time, and it was wonderful to see them. We all ate lunch together and went back to the hospital to see Eoin again before we returned to Cork that night. I was shell-shocked on the train home and had no idea of what would happen. It felt unnatural to leave him there and not be a part of the family. I wanted to sit with him and absorb every detail of him into my heart and head. I was terrified.

I returned home to Aidan and cried for such a long time, expressing my need to go back to Dublin to be there for Eoin. He was insistent I return to Dublin the next day if that was what I needed to do. I went back early the next morning and Rachael was there to give me a bed and much-needed reassurance. I went straight to the hospital and up to Eoin. No change. I heard something that morning from one of the nurses that made me laugh. While I was sitting by the bed holding his hand, she came along and said, 'Oh, you must be another sister – you two look so alike.' Her words gave me comfort that morning for some reason. I bumped into the gang in the cafeteria, and no one seemed too surprised to see me there.

Later that night, thankfully, Eoin began to regain consciousness. Though the pressure on his brain was still much too high, at least he was awake. Those few days were a blur for him. Paul, his friend, and I spent the next day with him. I thought that maybe Eoin would not know who I was – after all, I was only a recent addition to his family. But no, he saw me that morning and said, 'Howaya, Claire!' As it turns out, he has no recollection of that day or some of the following ones and certainly has no memory of the accident. It became clear that he would be all right – some changes, perhaps, because of the knock on his brain, but the same lovable rogue was back with us. All that mattered during that time was that Eoin was going to be all right, and all of my stupid and inconsequential insecurities were pushed to the side. I loved this family and was blessed to have found them and be accepted by them, and that was that. Time to move on and learn to trust them for the kind and compassionate people that they are.

Mary and Breda shortly afterwards gave birth to two beautiful baby girls. Kieran and Lisa have since made their first holy communions. Twenty-firsts, birthdays and Christmases have come and gone. Some I can make and others I cannot. There are certain occasions that I need to be part of to here in Cork, apart from the craic I would miss if I was not present for them!

It's not possible to be everything to everyone, and I think that both families know that and don't take offence at my not being able to be there for a birthday or a celebration at times. It's not easy for Kieran and Lisa, now ten and eleven, to understand why I am not with them on certain occasions. They have also begun to ask questions about Cork and why I am down there and not in Wicklow. I answer as best I can and give them lots of hugs and kisses. Children are so accepting and I never gave them enough credit for how much they can understand and appreciate.

Slowly, most of us began to communicate again, though at a slower pace, and Eoin began to improve. A year ago another milestone came and went. Mai, Breda and her little girl spent a night or two in Cork with me in our home, as Aidan had gone to the World Championship Rally in Wales with the rest of the Wicklow gang. For the first time, I spent some time with a little baby and had my first lessons in how to feed and look after someone so young. Mai began to talk about the years before I came looking for her, about that letter I wrote and how it made her feel, and both myself and Breda gained a little more insight into how this had affected Mai. I had a chance to cook for them and spoil them in some small way, and I loved having them in my home.

I love it when they come to visit, yet try not to exert too much pressure, enquiring when they will be down again. I have learned some valuable lessons of late. To seem to ask too many questions, for example, is sometimes viewed with suspicion, not merely as a genuine interest in getting to know them. It is very difficult when I want to ask hundreds of questions of every one of them, as there's so much I have missed out on. They have grown up with each other and, despite being accepted by them wholeheartedly, I long to forge closer bonds with them, which could take years, especially from Cork to Wicklow. I asked them not so long ago to give me time and respect my wishes, and I too have to listen to what is said or unsaid and respect and value what they choose to reveal to me.

It is probably a little naïve of me to hope that one day the gap of nearly thirty years can be bridged, but our trust for one another grows with each passing week. I know that I have been blessed with their friendship, the likes of which we are rarely lucky enough to have in our lives. I hope to become a sister to them all eventually, where they will just arrive on our doorstep enquiring if there's a pint in the fridge. Aidan said to me recently that I should invite them down, again and again. But I don't wish to make them feel like they have to come. I hope that they know the door is always open and that we love to have them stay.

We have begun to talk about how they feel about my having come into their lives. Some have told me I am already their sister and love me as such. Others prefer not to mention it at all, just to enjoy each other's company whenever we can. I am happy with whatever I can get. Do they feel anything for me other than friendship? It's hard to say. I like to think so. A funny story helps me believe that love is possibly growing already.

Our drains collapsed a year ago, and when Joe heard about the problem he insisted on coming down with Paul, a family friend, and fixing the drains for us, rather than us spending a fortune trying to find someone to fix them. We met them on a Saturday night, and we had a hard night of it. Bed at 6 a.m. and up again at 8 a.m., heads a bit worse for wear. Mid-morning, a problem was discovered and part of the existing drain had to be cut with a saw in order to progress. Unfortunately for Paul, he was standing directly in the spray of the sewer pipe, and when the drill managed to slice through the drain, the contents sprayed all over him. Joe and Aidan split their sides laughing while poor Paul emptied whatever he had in his stomach onto the gravel, and despite feeling so sorry for Paul, their laughter was contagious. It was a horrible job and I think their actions spoke louder than words – perhaps they care more for me than they let on sometimes.

Little gestures mean so much, like a little teddy bear bearing the words 'special sister', or being introduced as a long lost sister, or catching the smile in their eyes when they introduce me to someone and see that person's surprise. It's a very special relationship and one that must be taken as it comes. None of us can force it. An aunt said to me recently that actions speak much louder than words, and it's so very true.

Aidan and I spent a weekend in Wicklow during the summer of 2004 and, as the others had commitments or holidays, Aidan and I spent the Saturday night alone with Breda and her fiancé in the hotel, which was a rarity with such a large family. It was one of the few occasions where we really got to enjoy each other's company and to know each other a little better. Christmas 2003 also brought a night that still makes me smile. We decided to bring Pictionary up with us for New Year's, for the craic. When I explained the concept of the game, at first everyone looked at me as if to say, 'Right, she's lost her marbles!' Teams of two people pair up and choose a card per team; one person has to draw whatever the card tells them and the other person has to guess what it is – no speaking or hinting allowed. It sounds easy, but imagine getting the words 'funny' or 'loud' to draw, and they are two of the easier ones.

As the drinks flowed, competitiveness flourished, partners were swapped and the craic was mighty. Cheating was rampant and the laughter could be heard from outside, I'm sure. It was a special night, and afterwards Aidan told me it was the first night he saw Eoin, Mary, Breda, myself, Joe and J. R. together as relaxed as if we had all grown up with each other, shouting, laughing and accusing each other of cheating. Apparently, Joe and I kept digging each other's arms and laughing hard as we tried to duck away. A fun night was had by all.

I love visiting them and sometimes I wish I had longer to stay up there. I wish sometimes Mary, my sister in Cork, knew them better and trusted my love for her as my sister more. I would like them all to know Mum and Dad better, because I would love them to know more about this part of my life. Having been included in every aspect of my life so far, it can't be easy for Mum and Dad to know there are now parts of my life that I experience alone. But there are always some things in life that we would like to be different.

Life would be very boring if everything we wanted just landed in our laps. What I am learning is that I have to try and be less hard on myself and more trusting of others and their intentions. I have to try and be more open in my feelings and not be so afraid of getting hurt. We reap what we sow, so now I give as much love as I can and have begun to express this to them. So what if they don't feel the same? As I said to Joe once, after an impulsive fit of honesty, it can't hurt to know there's one more person in the world who loves him, right?

At long last, I have begun to listen to Mum and Dad and know that I don't have to feel guilty for needing to search for my roots and my birth parents. It's natural to want to know and to ask questions. I have changed so much in the past few years and have found a voice that is stronger than I ever imagined possible. I am more

tolerant and less tolerant: more tolerant in that I am able to understand why people say and do things; less tolerant of hatred, petti-
ness and selfishness, for these can eat away at you and turn what
was once a beautiful soul into a spiteful and hateful person.

I turned thirty in March 2004 and little did I think it possible,
years before, that on that night both families would join together
to share an occasion with me. It was as if they were making a silent
promise to share the next thirty years with me. It was an unusual
night for Mum and Dad, and also for Mai and Tony and for all
their family, for *my* family. However, for my sake, they took the
time to try and get to know one another and it was a special night.
It's time to grow up at long last, I guess, and I'm enjoying every
minute of it.

'Lord, grant me the serenity to accept the things I cannot
change, the courage to change the things I can, and the wisdom to
know the difference.'

Hmmm … I can always keep trying!

14

MOTHER AND CHILD

I have written about the younger members of the family and how far we have come. It was easier for us in many ways, as we really had no previous history, no preconceived notions. The possibility of their existence never entered my mind before I heard of them all those years ago. It might seem strange that I have not mentioned much about the woman who gave birth to me and then gave me the chance of a life so special and so loved in Cork. I have both her and Tony to thank for my mum and dad and for the love and security they provided for me every day of my life.

Eileen and Colum will always be my mum and dad because of the loving upbringing they gave me, nothing can ever change that. Mary will always be my sister, yet oddly there seems room for more siblings in my life. None of the gang in Wicklow, however, could ever replace the feelings I have for Mary, but I have enough love for other siblings in my life all the same. Perhaps it's because we are conditioned to accept only two parental figures in our lives, if we're lucky enough. As I had no expectations of the younger gang, it seemed easier to accept them as they were and for them to accept me also. It was simpler without any baggage between us. Maybe in some ways it was less painful.

The relationship between Mai, Tony and myself has been much slower. I really do not wish to diminish Tony's position as my birth father, but I think in some ways I have also begun to get to know him also a little bit better than Mai. He's open and very upfront about himself and the choices he has made. It is easy to accept him without any mistrust. He has been a part of my life for only a short time but I already have such a great respect for the man that he is. Mai is a very loving and strong person. I sometimes wonder at how she coped over the years. First she lost me as a baby to adoption, then she lost her son Liam to meningitis at age seven, and she must have suffered terrible heartache.

I am an adopted person and will be the first to admit I formed some very wrong opinions, subconsciously, about my birth mother when I was younger. Without actually letting myself form a picture of the woman who gave birth to me, I still had an idea of what, in my mind, she might be like. I compared myself to her, I suppose. I imagined her to be very strong, tall perhaps. As an angry young teenager, I believed that she did not love me, as she didn't care enough to fight for me. I presumed, that she was alone in her making the decision to have me adopted. I thought of her as someone who simply got on with her life, was maybe now settled with a husband, but certainly someone who, every now and then, perhaps thought about that little girl she 'gave away', wondering what her life was like. A silly term, 'gave away', as if to imply the mother did not care at all and discarded the baby.

This was the opinion I had formed of Mai before I even knew her name. It was either that scenario or that she had died and I would never get the chance to meet her. So I had prepared myself for neither the fact that there was a birth father involved, nor that Mai and Tony would actually be married – nor had I prepared myself for the person that Mai is.

It's hard to write about someone related to you by blood, yet not really knowing her at all. All I can tell you about is the person Mai is to and for me. Mai is stronger than I gave her credit for but with a vulnerability that she tries to keep hidden. I think she has spent her life supporting others and loving others and has maybe forgotten the ability to let others support her. She is a very warm, open and loving person and has a natural ability to draw others to her. I see her loving the younger kids, older kids, cousins and extended family, as if God put her on this earth for that purpose only. She has a lightening fast wit.

I am like Mai in many ways. I am terribly stubborn, though game for a laugh. I sometimes find it hard to take chances and I take the knocks in life hard, harder than anyone should. We are both inclined to be passionate in exchanges with others and have hurt each other in the past because we have not communicated properly. For all this, I still don't know her as well as I should. Nearly ten years have passed and until quite recently there were times when I still felt nervous with Mai. There is still so much to be said about the past and the mistakes we have both made. There is nothing Mai has done to make me feel this way – this is just the way I am. I wonder if she might feel the same at times.

Something began to weigh on my mind that made me feel uneasy, unsettled and upset. I talked to Aidan and we believed it was simply a matter of time before everything settled naturally. Some people might consider it strange for tears still to be a part of my life. After all, things seemed to be storming ahead – what exactly was wrong? That's just it ... I couldn't quite figure it out. I had at last accepted the fact that I loved this new family, and I hoped in time they would feel the same. But still something was missing, not quite right. This was one of the first times in my life that I did not turn to Colum and Eileen. This time, I needed to talk with someone who understood what was wrong, someone who had been feeling the same confusion, someone who could help me to understand what I could not understand myself. This person was Mai and, as it turns out, she had been feeling the same frustration at the pace we were getting to know one another.

I began to e-mail Mai and to communicate with her on a one-to-one basis about how I was feeling and how frustrated and confused I was. In many ways, I was asking her to help me understand what was upsetting me. I had a conversation with Joe too, and while he knew something was upsetting me, he didn't know the extent to which I hurt. I found it difficult to share my true feelings with Mai, because more than anything I did not wish my hurt to be an accusation or interpreted as anger towards her. It was just me turning to my birth mum, asking her to understand and to help me. She was able to offer advice, as only she could, being so close to the issues involved.

Mum and Dad were always a huge support and ready with open arms, yet they did not know what it felt like to be a part of another woman and at the same time to feel unsure of her. There was just so much that had been left unsaid, and when Mai and I had tried to talk about difficult emotions in the past, we had both reacted angrily. I was afraid of that happening again. After all, this was the woman I might have called Mum if different decisions had been made. Mum and Dad tried to understand. Of that, I'm sure. They tried to work out the dynamics between Mai and I and tried to protect me from hurt at every turn.

There were still some things, however, that Mai and I had to face up to. Mum and Dad loved me and that was enough. It's all I have ever needed from them. However, I needed Mai to understand what it is like to be an adopted child, and at the same time know that I don't blame her for it and am forever thankful to her for the love she ensured I received from my family. I wanted to be able to discuss what was going on in my heart with her, and I needed her to reassure me that it was all going to be all right, that we could both learn to leave the past behind and move forward.

Mai explained to me that, although we are all part of one another's lives for over ten years now, it was only for grabbed weekends here and there, often with much going on around us. The distance certainly makes it hard at times. There is no opportunity to drop in for a cup of coffee and a chat. She also made me feel comfortable, letting me talk to her about my feelings about being adopted. Once I found Mai, even though I had the sense to realise it can take years to grow to love someone, I still longed for the natural bond between mother and child to be there between us.

I was searching for the bond that is formed between mother and baby in the first few weeks in a baby's life, providing the child with a sense of security and warmth. For some strange reason I expected it to be immediate. That really was not possible. For this bond to grow between us, it will take time, getting to know one another, growing comfortable with each other's company and learning what it is that makes us who we are. I am learning, at long last, to let go of whatever notions I had of my birth mother before I had even met her. We are learning about one another now and learning how to move forward.

Mai said to me a few years ago that she can never be my mother, and it was a hard thing for her to admit – yet it is true. Mai told me that she can be like an aunt to me, and in time we could grow to love one another. I was happy with that, but now, as time has passed, I think we will be much more than that. I watch Mai and Tony with their three grandchildren and see how much they love them, as they did their own children. I now know they did not give me up to be adopted simply because they did not want the trouble, or from a lack of love for me.

So Mai and I are finding our feet. Through our emails, I have at last begun to open up to Mai about certain things. I am not afraid of letting her in any more. We have agreed to swap question for question, and we have told each other nothing is taboo. We are doing our best to answer as honestly as we can. I visit them when I can, and if it's been a few months, I feel the need to see them. I would love them to visit Cork more but realise that, like myself, they have commitments and busy lives. Their home is always busy, with people coming and going constantly, always with a comfortable, relaxed air about it. They would not have it any other way. The most special thing about our relationship now is that we are learning who we really are, faults and all, and I am no longer a novelty.

The excitement about being a part of one another's lives is passing, just as it does with any new relationship. We have quarrels, and more will come no doubt, but we continue to get to know one another. I love being a part of their family life, yet it is still difficult for Mai and myself to find time to spend on our own.

I was up with them one weekend in 2004, for example, and Mai and I had intended going for lunch somewhere on our own. For one reason or another, and to be honest, neither of us would really want it any other way, many others joined us for lunch and we had great fun. Mai and I sat together and chatted, about years gone by and the years to come, and whatever came up in conversation wih the others because Mai and I knew there would be plenty of time for us to talk about the issues between us.

What is important is that we have begun to laugh with each other, at each other's antics, and slowly we have begun to feel at home with each other. I know that both of us have learned a lot about ourselves and have let go of a lot of the pain and grief from our lives. I have learned that the past is gone and that it doesn't have to shape you or make you bitter. You don't have to let that happen! You can change, not the past perhaps, but you can shape the person you become in the future. Because of this I am becoming a better person, more able to be honest with others and to be myself with Mai.

After a weekend in Wicklow, when Sunday arrives, I always find myself with tired eyes after only a few hours' sleep. I guess I want to make the most of my time up there, but as a result my emotions run high when it is time to leave. It's not that I don't want to return to Cork, because my family, friends, and the life I have made for myself are all there. Without discounting the wonderful life I have in Cork, in Wicklow I feel a freedom. I have learned about those first few weeks of my life and I seem to be able find peace there. My blood quietens when I'm in Wicklow. I consider it to be another home and I love my family there.

As time passes, I get to know their friends and they get to know me. I am completely relaxed in Wicklow and as much myself as anywhere. I feel comfortable enough to be myself, both good and bad, with the knowledge that I am accepted for just that ... for me. It's a great feeling. As in Cork, I don't have to try to be anything I'm not, and when I'm with any of the gang, I am with family. I love to learn about what has happened in all of their lives. Mary Junior, remembered me with a beautiful gift from New York, as did Joe, which made me happier than they might realise. As I live so far away, any time I visit them we are anxious to catch up, find out what's new with each other. Mai enjoys the banter, yet sits quietly for the most part, watching our antics, smiling and happy that we are all together.

On a recent Sunday, when it was time to leave after an action-packed lunch with all of us around the table, I felt the usual melancholy set in. When I am impatient to know everyone as well as they know one another, it is hard to leave for Cork again. This Sunday, Mai knew I was quieter than usual and followed me out to the car. It was a miserable day, raining, chilly and damp. We sat in the car, opened a packet of cigarettes and rolled down the windows. We talked for hours, about Mai's life, about mine. We shared confidences with each other and were comfortable in each other's company. We laughed, we cried, we gave one another honest opinions about particular problems and, in my eyes, it was two people, who are very similar, sharing experiences and enjoying one another's company. It was a great few hours, and driving home that evening I felt a peace settle within me. This was the first time that I did not cry driving home from Wicklow, thinking already of the next time I would be able to visit.

On the way home that Sunday afternoon, I let go of the past a little bit more. I drove home thinking about them all, and instead of a small part of me regretting I did not grow up there, with a sense of what I had perhaps lost out on, I simply thought of the great shared experiences that lay ahead and thought how lucky I was. This sense of expectancy was like nothing I had experienced before. This was not just a sense of looking forward to something: what I experienced was sheer joy at the possibility of sharing this family's life. I had the answer to the last question that haunted me: I was already a part of their lives and would remain so for the foreseeable future. I was elated that afternoon, truly elated. I have always been impatient waiting for special events to arrive – birthdays, relatives returning home, Christmas – simply bursting at the seams for it to happen. Yet the sense of looking forward that I had that afternoon was different, life seemed full of promise, as if things had finally fallen into place.

I know now, without a doubt, that we already have a great bond and this will get stronger as time passes. I wonder whether they realise they have given me such an amazing gift? It's easy to get to know someone when there might be shared interests and a similar outlook on life. But everyone in this new-found birth family has accepted me as a family member of one sort or another, and I know many of them consider me a sister already, with all that that entails. Some of Mai's and Tony's brothers and sisters even remember me at times with letters and news, including me in their day-to-day lives. Their welcome has given me back a confidence and acceptance of myself.

I spent years believing that I had to be someone I am not, that I had to be invincible, tough, the best at anything I attempted. I believed I had to achieve, to prove my worth at home, at school and in any other aspect of my life. Maybe maturity has taught me a few things along the way, but I also believe the gang have taught me much about myself. I'm not as afraid of new situations or the unknown any more. Of course, each experience in life has the possibility of things I am not prepared for, but this does not terrify me any longer. Life offers you happiness and sadness and we have the ability to overcome most things. It's how we deal with the challenges that life throws our way that makes us who we are, not what happens to us along the way.

I have realised that I'm not defined by the fact that I'm adopted. I don't have to feel ashamed of that and I don't have to try and be someone I am not. Like anyone else, I have my good points and my bad points, and I'm beginning to realise that I am what I am and I actually like the person I have become, especially these past few years. I have begun to grow comfortable in my skin.

My family in Cork started me on this road and loved me as much as any human being could, but what this new family have given me is the story of those two months before I became a Cashin, that chunk of my life when I was, in fact, very much loved but circumstance dictated what was to happen next. To put it simply, everyone at some stage, I'm sure, has experienced what it feels like to love someone and to realise that their love is not returned. That's what the first two months of my life meant for me, that my birth mum did not love me, before Mai and Tony showed me otherwise. It made me hold back from relationships, without truly loving people who tried to care for me, afraid of any love they offered.

It's time for not only myself but also Mai to let go of the past. The past does not define us, but the choices we make and how we lead the rest of our lives can shape us and the type of person we choose to be. I really look forward to what's ahead and to many special relationships with mutual respect and love. In an ideal world, I would love for all who shape my life to know one another. I am loved by so many people and I know what amazing characters they are, so full of love, humour, openness and a passion for life and all it has to offer.

My families in Cork and in Wicklow have such an amazing capacity to love, and it would be nice for them all to gain some insight into one another's personalities. I think that if we were to get together for an evening, they would all enjoy each other's company enormously. Maybe that's one of the things about growing up I still have to come to grips with. I guess there will be people who might become part of my life that my family here in Cork might not know all that well. That's something that I will have to come to terms with and accept in time.

Since I began to tell the story about how I came to know my family in Wicklow, almost a year has passed. A lot has changed since then. As I began to write this, I asked a lot of questions of people, many of them in similar situations to myself, either about to embark upon a search or having completed one. Each one of them had a similar story to tell. Once an adopted person makes the tough decision to start searching for a birth parent, despite what may lie ahead, one thing is certain: the need for support – support from your family, support from friends, support from partners and, very importantly, support from the agency that instigated your adoption in the first place. The individuals who made such a life-altering decision as who was going to adopt you and where you were to grow up should have a role to play.

I agree with the essential principals of adoption. There will be times when a mother, for one reason or another, may not be in a position to provide a home for her baby, and adoption *can* provide a loving home environment for children. I have been one of the lucky ones. What is vital to remember, however, is that, despite a loving environment, the child may still experience a spectrum of emotions as they begin to mature. Some may only have a sense of curiosity about the facts surrounding their adoption, while others, like myself, may feel a torrent of emotions that can be debilitating for a while and absolutely suffocating.

Adoption agencies must be open to any adoptee approaching them for news or information in a Christian and understanding way. It is our right. Once an adopted person takes the step to contact the agency involved, they should be given the opportunity to speak with someone qualified and experienced in search and reunion procedures. At each and every step of the way, and for every person that is touched by the adoption process, there should be a support network, preferably from those who have experience of dealing with the very real and raw emotions of the adopted person, the birth family and also the adoptive family, and in this way they may be able to help with preparing them for what might lie ahead.

I strongly believe, also, that the adopted person should be given a time frame of how long, realistically, the agency expects the search for information to take and for that agency to maintain contact with the individual at every step of the way.

Once the bombshell of information was dropped on me that day at St Patrick's in Dublin , I heard no more from the society or from anyone within those walls. My family, myself and the gang in Wicklow were left to our own devices, to try and make as much sense as we could of the feelings that nearly drove me insane. Mai also had difficulty in trying to make sense of what had transpired between us. I grappled for a long time with anger and confusion and seemed paralysed at times. I was incapable in the earlier days of uttering words that made sense of what I was feeling.

This is simply not good enough. I have written this book for a reason, and it may well raise a few hairs, but I feel passionately about adoption and what a gift it can be for all parties concerned. It deals with such an inherently moral issue that, when faced with the apathy of such a prominent adoption society, I find it shocking that any adoptee could be left without the proper support needed to reach the other side.

This book deals with my own experience of adoption and the difficulties I have faced. If a woman discovers she is pregnant now, I believe she has more choices. There is government support and, in many ways, society is more open to single mothers. With or without family support, or indeed support from the birth father, a child *can* be given a very rich and fulfilling childhood. I cannot, or rather will not, suggest one way or the other which is better for a child because, as in all situations, every circumstance will be different. Each woman will have to make her own mind up concerning what sort of life she can offer her baby. Each woman will also have to make the decision whether to actually give birth to the baby she is carrying or to terminate the pregnancy. Again I cannot and will not dare to comment on whether this is right or wrong, I can only comment that I believe it has to be the mother's choice. I know what my faith teaches me, but I passionately believe that it's not up to us to judge anyone in this life.

However when writing about my own circumstances, I do have the right to state plainly my opinions about adoption, my own experience of it and what, in my opinion, can be done for the future. I realise that much is changing. I'm sure anyone reading this can recall receiving literature through the post in 2005 concerning the new adoption register and a database where birth-family members and adopted children can input information, hoping to gain an insight into their adoption from one another and the degree of contact they desire. This is a start and every little step is a giant leap in the right direction. There is, however, still so much to be learned and changed.

Adoption in Ireland today seems to be changing from an essentially closed and final agreement, in the way I was adopted, towards a more open form of adoption practice. In a fully open adoption, the birth parent/s and the adoptive family know each other and have ongoing communication about the child. The frequency and extent of contact between birth parents and what society calls adoptive parents, and the communication that follows over the years, needs to be agreed and even renegotiated at different times in the lives of the individuals involved. The degree of openness and communication will usually depend on the comfort levels of the birth parents and adoptive parents over the years, and only a relationship which develops over time can accommodate this. After all, every person at the beginning of this delicate relationship will more than likely be strangers to one another and only time can tell how the relationship will evolve.

It is easy to understand how prospective adoptive parents would worry that the child might be confused about who his/her parents are, or indeed that the child will learn to play one against the other. What of their loss of privacy due to visits, if those visits are indeed welcomed, or what if the birth mother won't be able to let go of the child? These fears can be addressed early on in the relationship and ground rules clearly defined and re-evaluated, if needs be, with the help of proper conscientious guidance and support. Many adoptive parents might be uncertain about what the future may hold for open adoption, however with the post-adoption services becoming available to everyone in need of them, it seems to me any problem associated with open adoption can be addressed.

Literature on the subject states that open adoption allows for the birth mother to assume more responsibility for the decision to relinquish, and as a full participant in the placement and entrusting of her child to a known family, she is better able to cope with feelings of loss, mourning and grief. Birth parents may also be better able to visualise the family environment in which the baby will live, and this may relieve some of the guilt and uncertainty that accompany relinquishing a child. Adoptees' feelings of rejection by the birth parents can also be diminished, allowing them to accept the situation earlier on in their lives. The need for search and reunion is also eliminated, and vital background information, genetic and medical, is readily available. Initial fear of the unknown for the adoptive parents prevents fears over the years about what might be ahead, for what in some instances might be the cause of a negative effect on the relationship with their adopted children.

Without a doubt, adoption has affected both of our families. It has affected Mai, Tony, their family and ourselves. I know Mum and Dad have always felt very strongly about unanswered questions about my birth mother, in particular about why I was given for adoption and about my health history, and they were unable to answer any of the questions that were a cause of pain for me.

Long-term studies on the adjustment of adoptees to open adoption are few, however, especially here in Ireland. Even the most perfect adoption carries a weighty emotional legacy – the issues it can create and the life-long effect on the child's developing psyche. But an adoption is truly made in the heart and soul, and nothing can jeopardise this love that the parent has for their child. I understand open adoption to be about love, honesty and communication and to be child-centred. Mum says the love comes naturally, and as parents you promise to be honest and do your best for your child. This isn't going to happen unless as parents you make it happen, live it every day of your lives as part of the family unit. Making an adoption an open one might well bring children a secure sense of who they are and who they can become early in life, and what a gift this is. Open adoption must be more about an attitude than merely a practice and must be borne out of a desire to do what is best for any child, rather than just the obligation to do so.

For open adoption to be effective, everyone concerned has to understand that the primary reason for it is for the child. This means that, even if the relationship is difficult at times, each person makes an effort to work through the problems and is committed to the common love of a single person.

Following my adoption and the difficulties I faced in modern-day Ireland, my experience has been that from the moment a child is adopted, the process evolves. From the day the child is born to the moment this 'child' learns to put the past behind, the agency involved must lend its genuine support in whatever form is necessary. Any agency that cannot maintain a support system in this manner should no longer be allowed to offer any search and reunion service, and all files they hold should be given to an agency regulated by people who know what they are doing and understand the true dynamics involved.

We all have a voice and it's up to each one of us to use that voice when we believe strongly in something. I believe this whole-heartedly. It's simply not good enough that the involvement of any adoption agency simply ends when the adoption papers are signed.

The time for change has come.

15

HE WHO KNOWS ME

I referred earlier to the emotions that might affect an adopted person and those that had an impact on my life. While I have certainly learned how to deal with many of my feelings, I think it is important to add that all the worries, fears and self-doubt do not disappear once we reach adulthood. Sometimes, as with me, when feelings are denied for so long the insecurities can magnify as the years progress. Some adopted people or their families might be reading these last pages with a sense of scorn: 'I never felt or experienced that.' To them I say, I am happy for you, but many of us *have* experienced these emotions as part of our everyday lives, as part of our very being. It is inevitable if, as a child, we experience such emotional challenges that these innate problems carry over into adulthood.

It is commonly accepted that many adopted people hesitate in establishing relationships, as these relationships may be viewed as dangerous, and this was certainly true of me. This fear of rejection can also be seen in the workplace, where a fear of success or a doubt in one's competency or expertise can result in a reluctance to attempt anything that might mean failure. I can only wonder about the effect my younger years had on our family home – this fear of the slightest hint of rejection must have had my family at a loss as to know how to avoid triggering it.

Although a lack of trust in the permanency of relationships can bring about issues of trust, intimacy and the resultant need for distance from a relationship, I still yearned for the very thing I found myself destroying. This was matched with an anger for the way in which I believed the course of my life was changed as a baby.

As with most situations and problems we have to face in life, no person or situation is identical, and every individual will react differently to a set of issues and challenges. As a result, there are no hard and fast rules. The only advice I have are words I have heard from my parents for they have taught me much over the years and managed to provide most of what I desired and, more importantly, what I needed. To provide for the well-being of any adopted child, there are some guidelines that might be useful for parents.

However difficult it may be to understand, despite lavishing your child with love and care, you simply cannot take away your child's hurt. It is impossible, because they must first try and make sense of their own feelings and then work through whatever issues they may have. You can certainly offer support and reassurance along the way, but this has to be a journey they make for themselves. They must be allowed to do this, to be able to mature and stand on their own two feet.

Despite a perfect upbringing, filled with love, moral guidance, family values and days filled with fun, your child may *still* experience this pain and the feelings might still come to haunt them, if and when the dam is allowed to burst. This has *nothing* to do with their home and their love for you. It is simply a part of them, and the issues that may or may not need to be dealt with are a vital part of who they become and their ability to lead their own lives and form healthy relationships with those they love.

This may seem like common sense, but *never*, not even in the heat of anger, threaten abandonment. Despite being pushed to the limit of your patience and being tested time and time again by your child, this is *not* what they want or need. In the long term, this will only serve to increase anxiety and encourage more behavioural problems. Patience and love for the child, like that which I experienced every day of my life, will ensure they can eventually depend on you and trust your love for them.

Always try to understand how your child might be feeling. Never tell your child they are being dramatic or overly sensitive. Everyone has a right to feel, and most of the time these feelings will come from a very powerful place, from deep within. While your child, of course, needs to take responsibility for their behaviour, their feelings need to be acknowledged, respected and understood.

Encourage your child to try and accept themselves for who they are. Even though they are certainly a cherished member of your family, try not to have any expectations, especially those that might conflict with their true personality, inherited or otherwise. Their talents and uniqueness come from within so try and allow them to just *be*. There will come a time when they will have difficulty enough trying to understand who they are, not to mention trying to understand the person you expect them to be.

Never try to compete with this other 'mother' or to take her place. As Mum has told me time and time again, in life we do not own anyone: we simply try and love one another as best we can. You love this child, have nurtured them and protected them and given them everything that's true in life, and this birth mother is not competition. If there comes a time when your child feels the very real need to search, then know that the child can love you both, without sacrificing one or the other.

Even if you manage to live your life by these values, there may *still* be a great deal of healing to be done. There is hurt and there is pain and these impact everyone in the adopted child's life. My parents have taught me two important things: it will never be good enough merely to gain acceptance from others; ultimately I must learn to love and accept myself.

Loss that is not mourned can be debilitating, leaving one at the mercy of inexplicable, forceful and unpredictable feelings. My parents have taught me that understanding, acceptance, empathy and communication are just some of the gifts that can be given to any adopted child. These can begin the healing.

My parents know me well, but I have hidden much of the depths of my feelings from them in the earlier years. There has always been one person in this world who knows me, the real me. That person is Aidan Murphy. I could write about how I think my insecurities and fears have touched our relationship, but there is no better person to tell you about this than him. I asked him some questions (in an effort to offer advice to husbands, wives and anyone who might care for someone in their life who is adopted). These are *his* words, however, and I know they are from the heart.

Because an adopted person has possibly more 'baggage' than a person who is not adopted, it can be a difficult relationship. However, you will only find this out with time. Generally speaking, all relationships start off in a similar fashion – you meet, you start to go out together, spend more time with each other and get to know each other. You get to know all about that person's friends, likes, dislikes, education, values and their family. This, in my experience, is where the difference, and therefore the difficulty, lies. Before Claire had admitted that she had issues she had to examine, I learned only part of her personality, the part she felt comfortable with and not afraid of.

As time passed, it became clear to me that she was experiencing much pain and suffering, which was hidden from most people. It was also hidden from me for much of the earlier years until eventually it was too much for her and for our relationship to bear. However, it was stronger than Claire and it fought its way to the surface. I had to fight to make Claire admit to these feelings and to see that searching for her birth mother might help to answer some important questions.

In my experience, the difficulty is the issue of an adopted person's trust (or lack of) in themselves and how worthy they believe are of love. When Claire and I were going out first, she did some very strange things, things that were incomprehensible to me at the time. When Claire eventually trusted herself enough to tell me what was going on in her head, her emotions and consequent actions all made sense to me but it took a lot of patience and understanding for Claire and what she was going through. It's not easy to help someone when you cannot completely understand what is going on deep inside. Sometimes, in the earlier years, it seemed as if Claire did not want to be helped when, in fact, she craved my support and understanding but was afraid of giving in to her emotions for what they might reveal.

Claire asked me, 'What behaviour did you recognise again and again?' I would have to say anger, fear, lack of confidence and possibly resentment. I come from a very close family, and while we are far from perfect, I know where I came from, where my bloodlines lie, and to this end Claire had no answers, only questions which caused her emotional turmoil.

Through talking, over time, Claire's barriers came down, and she learned slowly that I loved her. Eventually, it became obvious to me that a lot of her anger was based in her lack of knowledge about her blood relatives and not focused towards me at all. With this understanding, I truly believed that she needed to search for her natural mother.

Claire asked me has she changed since the decision to search for her birth mother, nearly ten years ago now, and I would answer, as the person I fell in love with, no. However, since meeting and getting to know her birth family, I can see many changes, particularly in the last three years, most notably in her self-confidence and her understanding and acceptance of herself.

Claire and her birth mum and dad met nearly ten years ago now and her siblings and herself met for the first time on the October bank holiday weekend 2002. It was akin to watching a fairy tale unfolding before me, and as most fairy tales go, this one appears to have had a happy ending. It is a wonderful thing to watch a family who have never met one another before, to see them interact and bond instantly, it seemed, realising immediately how much they actually have in common. How much of this is due to the same blood that runs through their veins, I cannot answer, but it was an amazing thing to witness, to feel this pre-existing bond in the room.

Although meeting her family has helped Claire, there remain aspects of her adoptive personality, like the need for much affection in our day-to-day lives, that are a part of her to this day. This may never change. Whether this is a result of being adopted and a need for reassurance or a result of just being a loving and touchy-feely personality, I may never know: it is the just the way she is.

If anyone reading this is considering a search of their own, one piece of advice I would like to offer, after my own experience, would be to have someone you can share the burden with, be it a partner, friend, family member or counsellor, because, as Claire says herself, it would be very difficult to go it alone. Try and heed the advice you get, no matter how irrelevant it may seem at the time – you never know when it might come in handy. Chances are that the search process will be different for everyone, and what might suit one person might not suit another. My advice to Claire was to take it slowly, yet she rushed headlong in and became very disillusioned with the process. When she eventually stepped back, slowed down and took stock of the situation, things became more comfortable and fell into place. The rule of thumb should be: you are the only one who knows what pace you are comfortable with, so don't be afraid to take advice, yet at the same time let your feelings be known.

One of the last things Claire asked me was whether her decision to search has been hard on me. Personally, it was not difficult at all. It has helped Claire immensely and that can only help us in our day-to-day relationship. I could understand that a partner might feel threatened by any prospective new family members, but my advice would be as follows. Have empathy. It could be you!

These words are written by Aidan, someone who has witnessed the angst from those early years and everything since. As an adopted person who has been lucky to have Aidan support me much of the way, I can give this simple advice to anyone hoping to be there for anyone who is adopted. As Aidan did for me, do not pressurise them into talking about their feelings until they are really ready.

Always be there with the reassurance, again and again, that your love for them is secure, no matter what may come. Listen without judging and try to understand where they are coming from, while being courageous enough to state some home truths at times. My behaviour in earlier years and my anger towards Aidan was just not good enough. I had to learn that taking my anger out on him wasn't right. In effect I was trying to push him away because I was afraid of trusting him.

Above all remember, as with most relationships, trust is a delicate thing. Once it is lost, it can be very hard to get back, especially for someone who has taken a long time to truly let the barriers down and give themselves completely, to trust completely.

If you are an adopted person and have some real fears about

letting go or letting someone in all I can say is this: just love them and let them in to see the real you. Don't be afraid of who you are, because relationships can be hard enough at the best of times. You need someone at your side that can accept you for who you really are. In order to give completely to one another, you must first accept and love yourself truly. Until you have learned to do this, you cannot really know who you are or, more importantly, what is important to you in life. It's also true that if you love someone, you should set them free. If they return, it was meant to be.

These last lessons have been the hardest to learn, not only for myself, but also for Aidan. I have truly realised what a fool I have been. My family never asked me to be something that I am not – they simply wanted to love me and care for me. My happiness was important to them.

With this acceptance of self has come the ability to look in the mirror and truly *know* the person that stares back. This has meant I am no longer able to lie to myself, or to others, no longer trying to mould myself into a particular person to make them happy. Most importantly, this has forced me to understand not only who I am, but also what is important to me in my life, what values I hold true, what expectations I have. I have come to realise that I have the right to say yes or no, and I have given myself the permission to live my life according to the values and morals that are essential to live my life as best I can, to be true to myself. This is what makes us all individuals and what makes life what it is – a challenge, certainly, but it can be true. I have learned how to live *my* life and not someone else's.

So, I've changed a great deal, or maybe I haven't really changed, only learned how to be happy and be honest with myself. None of this has been easy for either of us and during the past few years Aidan has been learning if he can love this person. He has dealt with it in his own way and in turn has made decisions that will make him happy. He is living his life and being true to his own beliefs, values and morals, which unfortunately are poles apart and will take us in different directions. The last number of years, however, have taught us both that neither of us can try and be something, try and change, in an effort to make the other happy. I have learned that first I must be happy with myself, and if I am truly content then perhaps I have a shot at making someone else happy, in time.

Aidan and I had a very honest conversation with one another in June 2005 because we care for one another's happiness. Although sad, we began to realise that we wanted very different things from life and have completely different beliefs. We could no longer continue to pretend, to ourselves or to our families. The decision was made that day to separate and try to piece together what it was each of us wanted from life. This is a story written for others, in an effort to try and help them, and although it would have been far easier to leave this part of my life out, it is important to be honest so that a lesson can be learned.

I have made other mistakes during the reunion process and hope that others can learn something because of them. My marriage to Aidan cannot be explained away with such a careless a phrase as 'a mistake' – I care for Aidan far too much for that. We consider one another true friends, but for anyone who has ever asked what is love, and for anyone adopted who finds it hard to commit to love, then these next words come from the heart.

Aidan helped me admit to much before we married and had, in earlier years, been supportive at each stage of the reunion process. I have learned, however, that I depended on him for this support but above all I have always wanted to marry, settle down and have children. This has been my one true goal in life – the need to have children, to create a happy home and find contentment and peace. But we did not truly know one another before we married, nor did we fully understand the way each of us wanted to live our lives. It is true to say that Aidan walked up the aisle with one person, but actually had yet to meet the person he was expected to spend the rest of his life with. I too had yet to accept this person who was to emerge. Indeed, I question if I would have been able to make that promise to Aidan that day, if I had known what was ahead, if in fact either of us had.

The home where I grew up became a refuge for me in many ways. I don't know if I would have ever made the decision to leave the one place I felt secure if my hand had not been forced. The first moment I was able to return home, I did so, and at once Aidan became my safety net, the person to whom I turned to protect me in many ways. He became my confidante and the person who knew my darkest secrets and worries. He was my best friend, and we will continue to love one another in our own way. I certainly don't have the answers to all my questions yet.

The only real truth I can offer is that we married at a time when my heart, mind and soul were in turmoil. I was unsure about what would happen between this new birth family and me, and to a large extent, I still tried to be someone for Aidan, to be the person who could make him happy. I think perhaps Aidan thought he could change circumstances too. When the dam began to burst and I let go of all the lies, there was no choice but to move forward and to be myself. Perhaps it was inevitable, reunion or otherwise, that I would find it so exhausting to keep trying to be someone that I was not. I had spent so long trying to be someone for others in my life that I lost the ability to look inside myself and ask what I wanted, and I hoped that someone would love and respect the person I really was. I figured that out eventually, and the person I wanted to be was not, Aidan realised, someone he could love. When we met challenges, the kind that I would have feared for most of my life, those that rock any foundation, I was unable to revert to past behaviours and pretend that everything was all right. It's very sad, not only for Aidan and I, but also for our families. But we are now living our lives for us, not trying to be something we are not for anyone else.

I do wonder if I am capable now of learning to trust someone else in my life, if I am able to learn from past lessons. If not, then I will have to cherish the love I do have in my life, whatever the source. Our families have said it has taken courage to make the decision we have made, but I don't think we are courageous – if we were, then we might have had the ability to look at our true feelings seven years ago.

The future, the unknown, is a little frightening, and I am unable to plan every move. I know, however, that I can't control everything in my life, but if I hold onto who I am and learn to be happy because of myself and not because of someone who cares for me, I'll be all right. I will be more than all right. I will find contentment and peace of mind. After all, if you don't truly love yourself, then what hope is there that you can love someone else and make them happy?

It's all new, and I can't wait to see what life has in store for me!

16

LIFE IS LIKE A BOX OF CHOCOLATES

I love those words from the film *Forrest Gump*: 'Life is like a box of chocolates. You just never know what you're gonna get!' No truer words were spoken. You're given a life with choices to make, some of them right and, unfortunately, as we learn for ourselves, some of them wrong. My choice to search for Mai (and as it turns out Tony), was the right choice for me and for Mai too I hope. I am a better person because of what I've learned about myself and those I love. I think even Mary, my sister, and I understand one another a little better. I know Mum and Dad have gained an insight into aspects of my personality that I have tried to hide from them in the past. I am blessed. My family were there for me at each step of the way, and every one of my new birth family have been so loving, open, welcoming and understanding. As Joe said, 'You really couldn't have wished for better – it's like something you'd read in a work of fiction!'

Someone recently asked me whether I would do it all over again, and would my decisions have been any different? I had to think for a few moments. Knowing what I know now, and looking at the mistakes I have made, I certainly would like to be able to start afresh with Mai, without anger and with a little more maturity. I would do anything to return to the night I wrote that letter to the gang, trying to explain things but failing miserably.

But we can't always rectify our mistakes, only learn from them. Having learned a few things along the way, I hope I'm a better person to know and be around. Knowing now what I did not know then about what is involved in starting a search, would I do it all again? That's not an easy question to answer.

During the last few months, I have tried to read as much as I can and research the whole issue of adoption. I had a conversation with Mum and Dad about my feelings concerning adoption and how the system works. I feel very passionate about its shortcomings and I feel it has failed many of the children, families and birth mothers over the years. What I did not realise is that the system, as I experienced it, seems to have changed somewhat and, with new legislation in the pipeline, I guess my Dad's opinion is relevant. He believes that no system, per se, is perfect and that to expect otherwise is naïve in some ways – one should almost expect imperfection.

I find this hard to accept. I believe that God gave us intelligence to be used, to question things and the way they are done so we can improve them and perhaps make life easier along the way for someone, anyone. Adoption deals with a little, defenceless human life, incapable of saying yes or no, unable to question the wisdom of someone else's choice. How can I simply accept that adoption, when viewed as a process, is not perfect? Not when the process of adoption decides what becomes of a child for the rest of its life. I was like many others, I'm sure, one of the lucky ones, and yet *still* the ghosts came to haunt me. What of those who have not had it so easy? What of their heartache? Perhaps some of it could be avoided if the adoption system was improved.

On the day I was born I was given to the nuns, where I waited, for six weeks, alone mostly, despite Eileen and Colum having been chosen from practically the first moment of my birth. From that moment until many years later, when I started my own search, there was no contact initiated from the adoption society. Over twenty years later, when I contacted them enquiring about my birth mother, I had to fight tooth and nail for the information I gained from them. I had to pester and call again and again until eventually I had to practically storm their defences in order to gain the information I needed. I *needed* this information – it was not merely that I wanted it! I then received my information in that very matter-of-fact manner and sent on my way.

The day Mai left the doors of the agency, before she was sent on her way, she was given a talk about morals and then expected to resume her life, to simply carry on and pick up the pieces by herself. My own parents, dealing with their own feelings during my search, were also left to their own devices, for the most part, to deal with things as best they could, to look to one another and our family unit for support.

Things improve because people strive to improve them. It is human nature to ask why. Systems and procedures are improved by an individual or a group's ability to look at something, ask what's wrong, take it apart and then piece it back together again. I believe in the love and principal of adoption. I believe in Eileen and Colum Cashin and their ability to nurture and love a baby as their very own. I believe in that baby's ability to love them in return as their very own family unit. But as a child becomes an adult and begins to reason and ask questions … where is the adoption system then?

I needed that adoption society to provide myself and my family with some answers, to convey to me that what I was feeling all those years ago was OK, to tell me that there were many others like me, experiencing the same emotions and confusion and that there were ways to understand and move forward.

What of my family in Cork? Was there anybody to provide them with information regarding others who have experienced their loved one's journey into the unknown, offering information and advice about how to support their child and how to under-stand their own feelings? I wonder at times how Eileen, Colum and Mary did it. What especially of Mai? How could she be simply left at the doors of the adoption society without a kind word or any real advice? Mai had to deal with her demons on her own. Tony loved and supported her, of that I am sure, but sometimes it is easier to gain solace from people who have had similar experiences. I felt only some of this hurt and anger when we met twenty-odd years later, and I found it very hard to deal with. I wonder if Mai might have been a more carefree person when she was younger if she had been given the help that she needed all those years ago.

Mai told me recently over lunch that she met one of the nuns a few months after we were 'introduced'. The nun enquired how things were progressing, and Mai tried to explain how we had not spoken in quite a while.

The nun said something like: 'Sure, the two of you are so alike, I had expected fireworks!' That was it. Those words were supposed to offer Mai solace?

Mum said to me one evening a number of years ago, 'Why can't you just let go?' I think she finds it hard to understand why I would want to collect my thoughts on paper and show them to the world. Again, I have simply this to say. In any situation in life, when faced with a problem, everyone turns to someone for advice, love and support. If only one person manages to find just an ounce of support from what I write, I can walk proud and know that that person realises they are not alone. I wrote this simply to help, to explain what might lie ahead. It is only one person's understanding, having completed the journey.

No. Things have to improve, especially when helpless children entrusted to the system are concerned. The government have taken the first courageous step and have begun to review adoption legislation. In particular they are looking at it with the understanding that the child's welfare is the most important factor. The Adoption Board, and more importantly the government, have seen fit to understand the importance of a trained individual meeting with the searching parties – first of all, to help them understand their own emotions, and then, perhaps, facilitating a first meeting and working together to help each party understand one other a little bit better. It is, after all, human nature that we turn to one another in times of great need. Obviously, there is far more involved, and for my part I had to admit that I needed help and had to listen to advice from others, but at long last it seems we have learned that adoption cannot simply end the day the adoption papers are signed and sealed.

Over the years, I have been guilty of sitting back and letting my concerns about adoption wash over me without taking an active interest in what can be changed. Everyone can access the information concerning the minister's discussion document and proposed bill, by contacting any of the government agencies or going online at www.irlgov.ie. Some aspects of this legislation pose many questions for me, which I have been informed by the Department for Health and Children I have the right to address. I can write to my T.D. outlining my concerns or I can address certain questions to the department itself. Particular aspects of the law in its present state certainly do concern me. Although I don't want to get too involved with the legal aspects of adoption, rights pertaining to the birth father cause me such concern that, I believe, not to give them attention would be a great injustice.

Right now, in the year 2006, the natural mother has constitutional and statutory rights to the custody of her child, while the 'non-marital father' merely has rights to apply for guardianship. He has other rights: his consent may be required in certain cases before an adoption consent order be made and he has the right to be consulted prior to the placement of his child for adoption, subject to four very important exceptions – that he cannot be contacted at all for some reason; that it is inappropriate to contact him; where the mother refuses to name him; or where she cannot identify him. Yet he has no right to *actually stop* the placement. If he does object, he has three weeks in which he can make an application to be appointed a guardian or the right to adopt his child. Yet the natural mother, by virtue of the fact that she is the mother of the child, has already been afforded such rights.

It seems today, as has been highlighted within the 2003 consultation proposals for change, that the few rights afforded the father under Irish law seem at odds with the approach taken under international law. There are many legal considerations, namely the lack of distinction drawn between the family life of a marital and non-marital family. International law also provides for the right of the child to know and be cared for by his or her parents, the right of the child to preserve his or her identity and that this access to family life is the right of the child.

During the 2003 consultation process, many views were considered – for example, that the father should have a statutory right to know he is a father, that compulsory registration of his paternity is acknowledged and that his name on the birth certificate should be a given. It was also considered that he should have the same guardianship rights as the mother and should have the right to be part of the decision to place the child for adoption. Like many other adopted people during the consultation process who expressed their frustration at the fact that a mother can choose not to reveal the identity of the father of her child, I fully support the changes that are being considered above. It was even suggested during this discussion that, should a natural mother not wish to raise her child, the natural father should be recognised in law as having equal rights to a marital father following a divorce or separation. In my mind, this has considerable merit. Yet this cannot be enforced here in Ireland without a constitutional amendment.

The questions that need to be addressed have to obviously

include what is in the best interests of the child, their wishes and needs, if applicable, the views of both parents and how agreement can be reached if different views exist. It has even been considered whether an independent mediator or 'defined arbitration service' should be established to deal with areas of disagreement.

The report being considered by government has now high-lighted and questioned whether it may be in the best interests of the child to be raised by his or her father rather than by strangers, except, of course, where there are welfare concerns. However, it is not considered practical to give a father automatic guardianship rights over his child.

What of a father who wishes to offer his child a good home and spare the child years of wondering why they were given up for adoption? Who has the right to say that a child cannot be given every emotional support, stability and love from its father? It is clear that much work lies ahead if equality of the sexes in this par-ticular area is to be achieved.

The question of funding, also, may have dire implications for the future, especially for those searching for information regarding their birth parents. Already the waiting list for search and reunion has reached a minimum of one year. The growth in demand for such a service has been significant in recent years.

Year	Number of Enquiries
1999	1,010
2000	2,059
2001	2,410
2002	2,617

While the allocation of additional staff is being discussed by the Department of Finance to enable the Adoption Board to establish a dedicated search and reunion unit, this new service and all adoption services will be based on the level of funding, i.e. the annual allocation, by the minister. What happens in times of cutbacks? Imagine the effect this will have on the minimum waiting period.

The system is far from perfect, but a start has been made to try to help people through the complexities of the adoption process. When my mind was in turmoil at particular phases of my search – my first meeting with Mai, my meeting with my siblings, the aftermath of each meeting – my emotions were akin to grief or loss. I eventually realised that I was not a victim and had to stop acting this way. I had the power to change things and to learn to become a nicer person. I learned that, in order to feel better, it is essential to let go of certain feelings and to let in and trust new emotions. It was a specific choice for me.

I believe that we have a long way to go, however, before we can be satisfied with even the modern-day structure of adoption. Only a few years ago, in 2003, the Irish government considered a piece of legislation that would instigate criminal proceedings against an adopted person for searching for their birth parents. In an age where we call ourselves compassionate I simply cannot find the words to express my disgust at such an idea.

Words fail me. Others in Cork were so impassioned by this news that they very courageously founded a voluntary group, aptly named, Know My Own. It was founded by an adopted person and an adoptive Father, who, because of his love and concern for his two adopted daughters, wanted to ensure that the preposterous proposed legislation was consigned to the rubbish bin where it belonged. Having had the opportunity to meet some of the Know My Own members during the past number of months it is obvious to me that this is quite a unique adoption support group, in that it's members not only consist of adoptees, but also adoptive parents, birth mothers, birth fathers, and siblings of adopted people, ensuring there is a great cross-section of views and experiences within the group. As a group of people offering sound, intuitive advice to many, the group seems to be going from strength to strength, holding monthly meetings in Cork, welcoming anyone who has been affected by adoption. That is the harsh reality of adoption. Not only can it affect the person who is adopted, but it can also have an impact on so many others, parents both birth and adoptive, brothers, sisters, husbands, wives and relationships of all kinds. This group offers support for all, hoping to share experiences, offer help with tracing birth family members and ultimately to seek changes to current legislation in Ireland. The Know My Own helpline telephone number is 087-258 4822 with an e-mail address of know-myown@gmail.com. Their motto, 'You are not alone any more', says it all really. I think if I had had such a network available to me years ago, things may have been a bit easier to figure out.

There are many facets to what is now being considered for the future of adoption. There is talk of freeing the flow of information for birth parents who wish to trace their children. The fine print has yet to be agreed, but an age between eighteen and twenty-three was mentioned. If I thought that Mai would have been able to contact me and access my details when I was that age, I don't know what my reaction would have been. My decision to search at age twenty-one was my own. I had some sort of control over the dynamics. I also know that, despite this, I was not prepared for the consequent flood of emotions that would swamp me. Whether or not counselling will be available in this scenario, I still feel that the decision to search and to let go of many ghosts, hidden for so long, must come from within and not because your hand has been forced. Obviously the birth mother or father also has rights, but it is vital that everyone in the reunion process wants the same thing. If one party does not want to continue a relationship, then this decision must be respected. It has to be said, however, that you never know how hot the water is unless you dip your toe, however tentatively!

I had the opportunity of asking 173 adopted people, over a three-month period, if they were glad they had searched. Five answers were available to each person who voted, ranging from 'Yes, it was more than I could have wished for' to 'Yes, despite the enormous pressures I felt' right down to 'I wish I had not started or completed a search.' Of those 173 replies, 95 per cent, despite pressures, difficult emotions and challenges, were all contented with their decision to search. I wonder what this group of people would have answered if they had not made the decision themselves, if they had been forced into looking for their birth mothers before they had admitted to themselves that it was what they really wanted, at a time, perhaps, when they were not ready to be compassionate or mature enough to understand.

Counselling is another vital part of the adoption experience, and knowing that others feel the same way can help you to understand your reasons for searching. Being able to speak with someone that I felt did not judge me for what I had decided to do, allowed me to hold on to my sanity and my sense of self. It gave me something to grab hold of – others have made it through, and so will I. It's a case of knowing you are not alone. I believed I could not share my deepest, darkest secrets and thoughts with my immediate family, as I felt that my search had caused them pain and I wanted to spare them any further hurt and worry, despite their protestations otherwise.

Your new blood relatives may have their own concerns and worries, and turning to them to help you understand your pain and emotions might seem as if you are blaming them, taking your anger out on them as a sort of revenge. So instead of being able to decipher each emotion on its own, figuring out what needs to be done and acting accordingly, you might lash out in confusion and despair. Until one day you realise that enough is enough and you need to ask questions and get answers from somewhere and quickly.

I was lucky my aunt and my family recognised the despair that became so hard to bear and helped me to talk with someone who had experience in this field and understood what I seemed incapable of expressing. I believe that this counselling stage of the adoption cycle is by far the most important and crucial and the one aspect that, up until very recently, has been sadly lacking within the Irish system. However, things are slowly changing. Support groups are now available where nothing is taboo, and a network is there to help you along the way, whether you decide to search or not. Sometimes it's just a matter of understanding your place in the world.

Mum and Dad spent a few hours with Joe and his girlfriend Sue recently in Monkstown, and while I was outside the restaurant, Dad shared his opinion that this search has been the making of me. While I realise it has provided a much-needed balm for the pain of not knowing why I was given up for adoption, what was, in fact, the making of me was having so much love and security as a child. Knowing that you are loved unconditionally is an amazing gift to give an adopted person, *any* person for that matter. Searching simply gave me some answers to questions that haunted me, and I was lucky enough to find more love in Wicklow. Not love that would replace what I had already, but a love that had the promise of giving me inner peace.

In years past, I may have worn my adoption around my neck like a noose and even used it as an excuse for behaviour that, while linked to some adoption issues, still hurt others unnecessarily. I have overcome so much and had to learn many lessons. A family member said to me recently that he is not sure if any adopted person can fully let go, fully trust and love with their whole heart. I can understand why he believes that, as adoption does certainly leave a residue. There is more to life, however, and I believe in taking chances and discovering what might be.

I used to believe that being adopted is not a good thing, that it can leave you with too many scars. My opinion has changed. Anything in life can defeat you if you let it. If I haven't already learned to open my heart fully, then I hope to learn how to do this in the future. In comparison to others in my life, I really don't have much to complain about. When I think of my family, cousins, aunts, uncles and close friends, many of whom have experienced great loss and pain in their lives, I wonder at times how they managed to put one foot in front of the other. Everyone has something they have to fight with daily, some aspect of their life that causes them to feel loss and regret and perhaps sorrow. It's all about how you choose to deal with that part of your life and if you allow it to define you.

So, would I do it all over again? I guess I would. Years ago, if I had been given a glimpse of the emotions and sheer desolation that I would experience, then perhaps I might have run in the opposite direction. Back then, however, I had no idea what I was capable of or how resourceful I was. I could not have survived were it not for those that love me, but I did not appreciate nor give myself credit for the strong person that I can be. My families, both in Cork *and* Wicklow, were able to give me that confidence.

Another piece of advice for anyone who is considering searching for blood relatives is this. Be sure you want to find them and learn the lessons this will inevitably teach you. It may offer untold sadness, perhaps that a birth parent has died and you have learned all that you are going to. Perhaps a birth mother never told her husband or family about that baby all those years ago. There is always the possibility that your arrival might be difficult. Prepare yourself well for every possible scenario. Although it might seem contradictory, if it's what you really want, then be as open as you can be and throw caution to the wind. This is your right.

None of this is as easy as it sounds, but with the help of those trained in this area, anything is possible. Be open to it, if you're ready. I was twenty-two when I first started this search, and I know now I was too young. I was not emotionally capable of understanding how my life and whole being were about to change. You can lie to yourself about who you are and your imperfections but the chance to change your future and the faith you have in yourself is in your own hands. You have the power to influence your life and become the sort of a person you *want* to be.

It is vital to understand, however, that if the search is truly what you want, then the waiting list is extremely long. In 2005, a woman working with Adoption Ireland explained to me the foundations of the new legislation and bill being discussed by our government representatives and the various aspects of modernising and humanising the adoption process. There is it seems, at long last, an awareness that improvements must be made to help everyone involved in the adoption process. This woman explained to me that, although Adoption Ireland are recognised by the government, until recently they only received a small contribution towards their running costs and most of the work and support offered was on a voluntary basis. Funding, however, is in the pipeline, and not before time.

You can join groups such as Adoption Ireland (www.adoptionireland.com), and each day on this site you can see this group of people support one another as best they can. They write about their searches and ask help from one another in finding information. 'Search Angels' do everything in their power to get them this lifeline, and as the process unfolds, in one way or another, this group of people are there for each other. Having reached the far side of my own journey and learned much about this very emotional process, I read words from adopted people on this site, asking for advice on issues such as contacting half-siblings, their first meeting, situations that are causing problems, and I recognise many of the feelings that haunted me a few years ago.

Everyone needs to change their perception of adoption and

their understanding of everyone involved in the process. A stigma is still attached to adoption; many do not understand it. Perhaps I need to accept that years ago, when I was adopted, the concept of counselling and the need to grieve because of adoption was not understood. Aunty Marie told me recently that the person you are at thirty and the person you become at sixty are worlds apart, that a maturity settles. Well, I suppose I won't experience that until I get there. Perhaps I will feel differently then.

For now all I can say is: if you feel passionately about something in life and your motives are pure, then don't just stand still watching life pass you by. Help others as they walk past.

They might be able to teach you something wonderful in return.

17

YOUR TIME HAS COME

If you believe wholeheartedly that to search for your birth mother is what is right for you, then enlist the help of anyone you can. I have already mentioned the need to trust those who love you and to take heed of their advice, they have your best interests at heart. Contact the agency from which you were adopted and enlist their help in your search. Do not accept any reason that they offer for withholding information if they have the records available. This is your right! I have heard stories over the years of people who contacted agencies in Cork only to be told that to search for their birth mother would do them no good. No one has the right to tell you this. You are the only person who has the right to make this decision.

The Adoption Board have told me it is possible to contact them if you want help with any matter and not to hesitate if you have a complaint to make about any agency. There are many organisations, previously mentioned, that offer advice for adopted people and can provide assistance from people who know what they are talking about, having experienced much of it themselves.

Perhaps you are a strong enough person to undertake this journey alone, and I admire you greatly if that is the case, but many societies now offer advice from people who understand what you are feeling. Don't let this opportunity for understanding pass you by simply because you do not believe in counselling and what it can offer or help you achieve. Don't knock what you have not experienced for yourself. If others can help you to understand the challenges and fears that this process might hold for you, then that is a good thing and invaluable for your peace of mind. Maybe this help can be offered by a close friend or family member – just don't go it alone. Everyone needs a shoulder to lean on.

I am not trained and cannot pretend to know precisely what words of advice to offer about what may be ahead of you, but I can speak from experience and the mistakes I have made myself. I have learned a few lessons the hard way, and have hurt others at times. All participants in the adoption/reunion process would do well to try to reserve judgement about one another. It's easier said than done, of course, and I have been guilty of judging Mai and Tony, for example, for marrying shortly after I was adopted. But your wish to search is a natural thing. For me, it was as if I had been holding my breath for many years, and having learned much from my new family, I found I could begin breathing again, deep, cleansing breaths.

The release of tension I experienced gave me a new lease of life and helped my understanding of everyone I loved, improving my relationships with family and close friends. Understanding and, more importantly, listening to others and what they have to say, or what is left unsaid, can help you to gain an insight into the reasons behind things. Agreeing with something and understanding something are two entirely different things. There are times that, while you might have made different decisions, you cannot judge someone because they did not do what you would have done. If you care for someone, you will learn to accept them as they are. That is what Mai and I are learning to do for one another.

Any person involved at various stages of any adoption process may have been hurt in some way. Your birth mother may have suffered over the years. You will have distinct opinions about what it is to be an adopted person. Your family and extended family members, all of whom you have grown to love and understand, may have strong feelings about your need to search. We need to try and understand one another and listen to what is said and, more importantly, to try and pay attention to the underlying emotions that may never be voiced. The strength of the emotions and suffering of many people involved in this process make the dynamics of any reunion, and perhaps just gaining information, such a delicate and unpredictable thing. Again, there are no hard and fast rules.

You, as the adopted person, obviously have the most compelling reason to search. Birth parents, in time, may also have the opportunity to search, but they must always be respectful of one another's feelings and reasons for particular behaviour. However, a birth parent or an adopted person should never, *under any circumstances*, search or contemplate establishing an early relationship if there is any possibility at all that it is not what they truly want. It could be very damaging to give hope of a blossoming relationship if this is not what you ultimately want. From the adopted person's perspective, for example, if there is even the smallest possibility of what might be perceived as another abandonment, then the birth mother should be honest from the very first moment. A second abandonment is almost as devastating for an adopted person and they will be much more conscious of it when they are an adult. This fear of a second abandonment (what if she doesn't like me or want me – what if we don't get on) is much of what stopped me searching in earlier years.

Any mother, or indeed any human being, can surely understand these fears. Some birth mother's may well want to 'leave well enough alone'. However, I believe passionately that when you give your child up for adoption, they do not have the ability to make you change mind about the future. You have the right, obviously, to make your own decisions about the course your life will take. However, this baby had *no choice* about what was to become of him or her. To this end, I believe that you *do* have some obligations to this child. This child, this adult, has a *right* to some basic information about the circumstances surrounding their adoption, possible lead information about the birth father and information about your shared medical history. This should not be denied to them.

I can of course understand the sensitivities and hurt that a birth mother may have in her heart, but this child needs this small part of you, to be given a permission of sorts to feel what they may be experiencing, to possibly quell their confusion and pain. If any human being can do this for another, then surely it is not too much to ask? I have learned of many situations where the elusive birth mother figure wrote to her 'natural' children after many years apart, only to inform them she wished to be left alone, that she had rebuilt her life without imparting knowledge of this child given up for adoption. This *is* the birth mother's right. But I believe her responsibility lies deeper.

If it is at all possible, it is far more loving and caring to meet once with this child and speak with them, explaining your circumstances and wishes. Allow them this one chance to question openly and search for their answers. Treat this child you gave for adoption with the respect and tenderness they deserve. After this, if you so wish, then make it clear you want to go on your way, but at least the child can then try to piece together what they can and try to make peace with the past.

When I consider my own dealings with Mai, subconsciously I think I needed to lash out, to hurt her, even though it was not a conscious decision to do so. Mum and Dad 'saved' Mai and Tony from a lot worse, I think, by trying to help me understand their decision all those years ago. It must have been hard for Mai and Tony to experience this but, as a result of the years of healing that followed and the example given by Mai and Tony, I advise birth parents not to give up, and no matter how many times this child that has come back into your life tries to lash out and hurt you, try to understand that it is just their fears and hurt you are experiencing. Show them that, no matter what they throw at you, you care for them and will always be there. Do not stop communication or contact – slow things down, certainly, and go at a pace everyone feels comfortable with – but do not abandon them again, for this will do untold damage for the rest of their lives.

When I met Mai and Tony first, I was concerned about what they expected of me, and they were unsure of what I expected of them, but there is no quick fix and everyone's experience is different. If as a birth mother your expectation is that your long lost child has returned, then this may be a lot for the child to bear, despite being a fully grown adult. When Mai told me that our relationship might develop akin to that which an aunt experiences with her niece, I remember the relief that flooded through me. Much of the worry and pressure I had felt since learning about them left me that day, and I am thankful to her for that. Mai and Tony were very open about the love they felt for me. They managed to lessen the load for me that day, and since then, a love has grown inside me for them both, for them all. The love that I feel now was not instant and it took time to grow. It is still growing, and I feel very protective towards them all already. I would defend any one of them, if I needed to, without a moment's thought. This would be my natural instinct. But this has taken a long time and has taken much learning about myself and trust in their feelings for me. What will be will be, and every person on this journey will have to try and understand one another and their own limitations. Issues will eventually be resolved but it is a slow process.

Try not to do as I did, in fact we all did – try not to rush things and make up for all the years lost. That's simply not possible. Try and build new relationships with one another, as adults, as the people you have become. Those lost years can *never* be recovered, and a birth mother will eventually have to mourn this loss and grieve, as will the adopted person. Unresolved grief, anger, blame and guilt can paralyse each party in the process and stop relationships developing, perhaps forever.

I have asked Mai how the years since I became part of their lives have been for them, in the hope that she could offer some advice for others in her shoes. Perhaps we are in very different places and have learned about this process at a different pace, but the following offers an insight into Mai's true emotions.

Hi. My name is Mary, 'the birth mother'. I find it very difficult to put my thoughts and feelings over the years on paper, but I will try.

I found myself pregnant and the only person who knew was my boyfriend, now my husband. I came from a loving family with five brothers, and I felt I could not ask my mum and dad to look after another baby after rearing six of their own already, during hard times, since there was no way I could look after a baby myself. In hindsight, I really should have told them, and I am sure they would have stood by me, but I felt I could not bring such shame on them. Thinking back, I deprived grandparents, aunts and uncles of the joy of seeing a beautiful little girl grow up in our family, not to mention the heartache I felt all those years.

I was six months pregnant when I first visited hospital. The hospital arranged for me to meet with a social worker, and between us we decided adoption was best for the baby if I was unable to tell my parents. My boyfriend had been in an accident, so marriage was out of the question – at least, it was not suggested to me – so I felt I had no other option. I was taken into hospital with a kidney infection and they treated me well. They kept me in a ward where women were in for operations, so when my family came to visit I was in bed and no one suspected anything. I went into labour three weeks early and Claire was born. I was told that as I was giving up the baby for adoption it was better not to see her, so she was wrapped in a blanket and taken away. To hear your baby cry and to know you are not going to have any part in her life is the most awful feeling you could have.

When it was time to leave hospital, I was brought to St Patrick's Guild, the adoption agency, and I signed some papers. It was like I was in a dream, as if it was happening to somebody else. I was given a lecture by one of the nuns on how to behave and told to get on with my life. They said that the baby was going to people who would love and care for her. I went home living a lie and my heart felt as if it was broken in two. I changed from a fun-loving young girl to a girl who had part of her missing. That was how I felt all those years, wondering if she was happy, wondering what she looked like, did she look like any of the other children when I had them.

I was brought back to sign more papers in a few weeks, and when I asked about Claire, I was told they could not tell me anything. I often phoned over the weeks, months and years and always the same answer.

When I was very upset, I was given the number of the Samaritans. I only wanted to know if she was safe, if she was in Ireland. I was not going to cause any problems for the adopted parents – I just wanted some news of her to put my mind at rest.

I still cannot complain too much about the treatment I received. I was looked after well in hospital and, in fairness, I suppose the adoption society could not give me any information on Claire's parents as this was the law set down by the government to protect parents of adopted people. If only they had said, 'Yes, she is adopted in Ireland and is happy,' that would have been enough. I knew that I would never see or hear from her unless she decided to look for me, as I had no way of getting in contact with her. You can imagine the joy and shock I felt when the adoption society phoned and said that Claire had been in touch and would like to meet us.

We arranged to go to the adoption society and the nun had a letter and some photos for us. It was like a dream come true. We exchanged letters and she was told I had married her dad and she had four brothers and three sisters. I was still living a lie and had to deal with telling the rest of the family that they had another sister. This went on for a long time, as I felt they were not the right age to learn something like that. I was very stupid – I should have told them in the beginning. We arranged to meet for the first time in March 1997 in Waterford. I didn't sleep a wink the night before – I was so scared of what she would think of me. We exchanged news of our two families. I was in shock and hardly knew what to say but Tony and Claire got on great and the evening went well.

Things did not go well between myself and Claire for a while. After years of this I had a chat with Aidan and I decided to tell the gang here and then my own brothers and relations. They were all great about it, and I don't know why I didn't tell them years before.

The children all arranged to meet one weekend in October. Claire intended to meet the older ones in the family, but they thought it would be great if Dad and myself, along with the two younger ones, turned up as a surprise. This did not go down well with Claire, as she wanted the five older ones to meet with her family first. I could not understand why everything had to be arranged just so. The day went OK, Claire's mum and dad and sister were really nice to us, but to be truthful, knowing we were not wanted put a dampener on things for me. I decided to stay in the background from then on and let the others get to know one another.

A short while after this meeting, the gang received a letter from Claire saying things were moving too fast for her and she wanted to slow things down, or words to that effect. That was fine, but it was giving advice to them about their mother needing help, acting like I had found a long-lost daughter, and that she would always be a Cashin and not one of us, which caused offence to me and some of the others. There were other stupid things in the letter too, but they are best forgotten. Having gone through a pregnancy alone and done everything I could to see that the baby was looked after the best way possible, I did not think I needed any help at this stage. So this comment annoyed me a bit, but I let it go and did not respond. I did not need anyone to tell me she was not one of us – I gave up that right years ago and I was not looking for a long-lost daughter. I knew that she was Colum and Eileen's daughter and I hoped that one day we could be friends. Things were not looking too good at this stage, but thankfully things got better as time went on. We now meet regularly and e-mail one another often.

If I were to start at the beginning again, I think we should have taken things more slowly at first, with a mediator who was a stranger to both parties sitting in on the first few meetings. Maybe we should not have mentioned the rest of the gang until we got to know each other. Should we have written a few more letters and talked more on the phone before meeting? Who knows – everyone is different. When you put high-spirited people like Claire and myself together, there are bound to be clashes, but hopefully all this will bring us closer over the years.

I cannot fully appreciate how it must feel to live with the loss of a child through adoption, only that it must pierce the heart forever. Neither can I pretend to know the unresolved conflict and hurt that Mai must have experienced during the years – I can only understand my own. I know my own feelings affected my relationships with others, and so their feelings must have affected Mai and Tony in their relationships. But I guess we must all try and help one another and, in time, our honesty and openness with one another, and our love for one another, will help to break down any walls we may have built up around our hearts.

I tried hard ten years ago to try and understand Mai, as I'm sure she tried to understand me, but we both had a lot of demons. I think Mai must have felt that trying to forge a relationship with me was like walking on eggshells, afraid of what might happen next. I really wanted to be able to make sense of Mai's emotions when she found herself pregnant in Ireland all those years ago, but I did not experience the fear and the stigma attached to being asked to forget about the child she brought into the world, so I can't truly understand it.

The church and adoption societies considered it essential to continue the silence surrounding an 'illegitimate' pregnancy all those years ago, and after the child disappeared from the mother's life, she was expected to carry on and just forget about it. The mothers were left, in most cases, to deal with their own grief and pain at having parted from their children. I wonder how much choice any mother did, in fact, have before they signed the adoption papers? What other option was available when the alternative to handing their babies over was to be made to feel unclean and an outcast from society? For my part, in trying to deal with my own pain over the years, I tried to keep any hurtful feelings in a cast-iron box in my mind and always tried to keep the lid firmly shut. In this way I had the ability, though limited, to manage the pain within my own life. Mai also developed her own coping strategy, I'm sure, and the emotional turmoil was hidden from others in her life who did not know. Was she detached in some small way from them, even isolated from them because of this secret? As she says herself, she was living a lie with those she loved, unable to admit to these feelings for fear of opening up old wounds.

The unfortunate truth about reunion, although it has been one of the most joyous experiences of my life, is that the hard work of reunion only begins after that first meeting. Adoption and adoption reunion are based to some extent on loss, and unlike a bereavement where there is some finality, with closed adoption, as has been the norm in Ireland until recently, there is no closure. An intense grief is experienced by many people involved in the process. The power of these emotions can be hard to accept, this yearning for what has been lost and can never be retrieved. I certainly fought hard to control the delicate equilibrium of these emotions, and like Mai, once the reunion began to draw near, and immediately after that first meeting, the release of emotions swept over me and seemed as intense as it was in earlier years. Both Mai and I had grown used to practising restraint during the years, yet as our emotions burst forth, we were still expected to hold it together for the meeting.

Mai and I, despite our best efforts, had our own expectations and fantasies of what might be. My advice to anyone considering a reunion in the future would be that expectations are normal, but it is vital to be aware of them and important to accept and understand them for what they are. Expecting too much can damage this delicate, budding relationship. Mai and I were also lacking in self-esteem, and our ability to speak up and say openly what we wanted for this relationship, or to set boundaries from the start, was limited.

Neither of us knew what lay ahead, and because there was much ambiguity about when and how we would contact one another, a lack of trust in the relationship grew. Certainly, when I backed off

I hurt Mai, and even though it was what I needed at the time, it could have been avoided if I had been more up front with Mai from the start. I hurt her because of it. Then again, we each wanted the other to like us so much, we were afraid to be too honest, that we might frighten one another away.

Post reunion, you might also experience, as I did, the need to redefine yourself. Life, to some extent, before this had settled into its safe little boxes and now everything was turned upside down. It's very hard to understand how, after so long, this loss and yearning for what might have been was as intense as in earlier years. But these unresolved emotions lie still and fester until you can no longer control them. This reunion was the catalyst for a new time in both our lives and one that certainly was the making of me. We turned to our families to try to help us through it. We managed, to some extent, to muddle through without the guidance of a counsellor. While counselling pre- and post-adoption might never have changed the initial mistakes we made, I believe that it could have prepared us better for what was ahead.

The relationship between birth mother and child has to be one of mutual respect and trust, coupled with the need for independence. It will more than likely, in many cases, resemble friendship, and while either party may wish for a closer and more intimate relationship, it is vital to remember that what you wish for may be more than what's on offer. A reunion is, in essence, a meeting between two adults who do not yet know one another, and you have to start at the beginning. While it may also be very hard, the birth mother will have to accept the place that the adoptive parents may hold in this child's heart, and she must respect this and not cross the boundaries.

When considering the relationships I developed with Mai and Tony early on, the relationships with my siblings were easier, and this can often be the case. This is not because you want to get to know your siblings more, merely that these relationships seem not to be as loaded. There is less history, and at times it is easier and simply about having fun. Mai and I both had different perspectives, but as time passed we tried to understand one another's priorities and to become more honest not only with each other, but also with ourselves. Clinging to the past does not help any reunion relationship. Instead, you must both try and look to the future and come to terms with what happened and how your own beliefs, expectations and emotions are helping or hindering your new relationship. For Mai and I, it has taken years, but there are many more ahead of us, thank God.

From my parents' perspective, only they can tell you about their own ghosts because of my decision to search. I think they realise now, after many years, that while it is possible to understand my experiences and fears during the years, they still cannot *know* them. I do not hesitate in saying it has been a difficult journey for them. Mum and Dad must have known that, in my reuniting with my birth parents, our relationship would change forever, and it has – but for the better. The love we feel for one another has not changed – in fact, it has strengthened – but any walls I had built up that acted as barriers to how I felt have collapsed. I am far more open and honest now when I share moments and memories with them, and that is precious. The great unknown during my journey must have been frightening for them and for Mary. Only with time can I show them that my love is as strong as ever for them.

One of the most difficult emotions you may experience during this process is the feeling of being torn between everyone. I felt guilty for such a long time. It suddenly dawned on me that everything was happening because of my decision to search. I felt caught between so many lives, and yet at times felt I wasn't truly a part of any of them.

I wish I could say it was easy to relieve this pressure and rid myself of the guilt, but I cannot. There was no quick fix. What helped me was that each and every person in this story had the ability eventually to look into their own souls and understand what they were truly feeling, feelings that never have to be denied or apologised for. More importantly, everyone directly involved in this reunion process learned that my decision to search was something that related to me, *my* needs, and had nothing to do with them or something lacking within our relationship. If each individual cannot examine the effect their feelings might have on a relationship, then these feelings of hurt and anger could be projected on some other participant in the adoption process. This can get in the way of understanding one another.

Before mature relationships can occur, a very long road must be travelled. An adult has to act where possible as a mature individual and, despite strong emotions, you must try and remain in control of your actions. While I might have felt angry at having been given up for adoption, and projected this anger on to Mai and Tony, I might not have been as in control of my behaviour as I should have been. Being angry was one thing, but I could have handled the anger better. Instead of keeping it inside and letting it hold me back, I could have been more open with Mai and Tony and voiced my feelings earlier, leading to a more honest relationship in the early days. Understanding your own feelings and taking responsibility for them can help the healing process.

My experience has taught me that, in the early stages of any reunion, it helps when the adoptive parents (a phrase I hate, as Eileen and Colum are simply Mum and Dad) back off and give any fledgling relationship an opportunity to develop without the adoptee having to worry about their feelings or their place in this new partnership. I needed 'permission' of sorts to be able to pursue the relationship with my birth parents, which was granted in their actions and unconditional love for me at every step of the way.

Mum and Dad taught me that everyone needs to provide understanding and support for their loved ones and never to pass judgement. Eventually, after I had begun to talk openly with Mai, it also helped that Mai and Tony accepted our budding relationship as one akin to friendship and placed it on a new foothold that meant less pressure. They accepted Colum and Eileen as Mum and Dad and we were able to move forward.

It must be natural and instinctive for parents to feel protective towards their adopted child, particularly if the newly arrived birth parent/s have difficulties handling the budding relationship. It's understandable that they might feel the need to step in to protect their child from being hurt. There is a huge difference, however, between supporting your child in these circumstances and getting involved – perhaps shaping the child's actions or opinions of the new birth parents. From the example of Colum and Eileen, all I can say is love your child, certainly, and offer advice, but leave any decisions to them – try not to force their hand. If you have an open relationship, they may well turn to you for advice, and their inner voice will eventually tell them what is right for them.

It is a slowly evolving process that takes patience, understanding, unselfish and unconditional love and the cooperation of everyone involved. While the following might be hard for any birth parent to read, it is essential in building a long-lasting relationship: an adoptee needs time to grow accustomed to the relationship, gaining faith and trust in it, slowly. This is not to suggest birth parents do not have a right to feel these emotions, but that they allow these feelings to develop slowly and express them only when everyone feels comfortable.

Eventually I realised I had to make some direct changes, some easier than others, before true healing could begin. The first change was to stop feeling like a victim, powerless to change anything. I wanted, and more importantly needed, to rid myself of this destructive belief. I realised that, despite everyone's best efforts, I had to take an active part in my own healing process.

I'm still learning and have to battle with some deep-seated beliefs at times, more so than ever because of recent lessons. I still find it hard to take risks. Until very recently I calculated every decision and the possibility of succeeding carefully. I found coping with mistakes very difficult, viewing these as flaws rather than simply mistakes that I can learn from. These were not life threatening. I need to free myself of the constant need for approval and the concern about what others think of me. These hold me back, or rather I hold myself back. In reality, we don't need everyone to love us – we don't even need everyone to *like* us. That's simply not possible.

What we do need to know is that we are real, and for the first time in my life I am myself, warts and all, and have come to accept myself and take pride in who I am. Nothing is going to change unless I make those changes myself, and every one of us has the power to do this.

I did not do this alone. I was taught by those who love me that you need a little help along the way and should not be afraid to ask for it. I simply woke up one day and decided that it was time I stopped denying painful truths in order to avoid making difficult decisions, decisions that would affect my well being.

18

FROM THE HEART

My search has been a blessing. But this story is not mine alone – it involves everyone in my life who has loved, cherished and cared for me, without a moment's hesitation. I know without doubt Mum and Dad would have given their lives for me if that was needed. They were my manna from heaven. The words that I have written, for the most part, have been my own experiences over the years, my own lessons learned, my own mistakes and realisations. Mum pointed out to me, having read some of the early writing, that I could not know how they were feeling as I searched for my birth parents – she maintains that they did not feel at all threatened. So I asked them to write their own words, words of advice for other birth parents looking for some direction. These are my mother and father's words:

We decided to adopt after much consideration over a number of years. Mary queried why she had no brother or sister. She knew that she had a sister who had died and could not understand why no one else was coming along. So we tried to find out as much as we could about the possibility of adopting a child from friends who had already adopted children.

Claire has asked us what the adoption process was like. It may well have changed in the last thirty years, but back then, the first thing we had to do was complete an interview with one of the nuns who called to the house. She enquired about our financial position and why we wanted to adopt a baby. She also questioned

Mary about her feelings. She requested letters from our G.P. about our health. Overall, the adoption society seemed concerned about the type of home and parents to which they would be entrusting a baby.

We left the decision of matching compatibility in their hands. We emphasised that when they had found a mother about to have a baby who they felt was suitable for us, regardless of whether it be a boy or a girl, we would welcome this child. The one fear we had was that the mother would change her mind during the six-month waiting period.

We were given no advice on the day we collected Claire, but we were not really in a position to listen to advice at that stage of the process. As Eileen says, it was in later years, when Claire approached adolescence, that we could have benefited from some guidance. All we wanted to do on that day was get Claire out of there and home.

A public health nurse called a number of times to check that Claire was being looked after, and the nun who originally interviewed us called once again before we went before the Adoption Board to sign the final papers. Once the papers were signed, we ran like robbers!

Raising Claire has been no different to raising Mary. Certainly there might have been different behavioural quirks as both girls grew older, but we gave them both the same care and love.

When considering how and when to tell Claire that she was adopted, we believed strongly that the foundation of any relationship is the ability to trust one another. We felt that if Claire was ever to trust us, we would have to be truthful with her from the very start. We must have done something right – she was always a very loveable little girl. They both were special girls and we loved them both.

When Claire's teenage years arrived, we knew that she had difficulties and a lot of questions that needed answers. Looking back, however, maybe we did not realise how strong these feelings were and that they troubled Claire so much. Claire's adolescence seemed to be the same as any other teenager's – moody, troublesome and throwing tantrums sometimes; lovable, helpful and considerate at other times. I know Claire has always felt there should be more support available for parents who adopt a child, and perhaps more advice available when their child begins to question aspects of their adoption. Each person will certainly have to decide that for themselves, and it may be a consideration for the future with the powers that be in government.

Claire has asked our opinion about open adoption, which seems to be a possibility in Ireland today. In the rearing of any child with two parents, a united front must be shown on any decision that relates to the child. Rearing a child, biological or otherwise, is a full-time job and there is no training for becoming a parent. You are just in at the deep end and have to trust your instincts.

As a united front is essential, I feel that another influence, such as the biological mother having contact in earlier years, would make an impossible task for the adoptive parents and a confusing situation for a small child. What children need at this stage of their development is love and security.

We feel strongly that it is very important, if at all possible, for a medical history to be provided when a child is given up for adoption. When Claire had to have her immunisations, we had no medical history and had no idea if we should get the three-in-one or the four-in-one shot for her. We felt very worried about this and believed that we were letting her down in some way. Another time, we had to take her for emergency surgery to have her appendix removed in the middle of the night and were again asked for her medical history. We had to give the same answer. We felt at a loss as to what to do and the doctors were also at a disadvantage.

We feel that open adoption is not a choice we would have made as adoptive parents. We believe that in the rearing of a child there should be no influence from any other source, even the sort of influence that might be present from a favourite uncle, for example. Truth and communication from an early age is vital and a small child needs a secure and loving home. We believe that introducing another 'parent' at this stage could possibly result in insecurity.

However, a contact address should be kept, at the adoption agency and photos and letters could be exchanged until the time is right for further contact and perhaps tracing. When a child starts wanting to search for their birth parents, they are probably at an age to understand what they are doing and all possible help, love and support should be given. We always had the feeling that Claire would want to search for her birth mother, but we worried constantly that it would not work out to Claire's satisfaction. Your concern always will be for your child and avoiding the possibility of them getting hurt. We were behind Claire all the way and just watched as closely as we could without suffocating her. We looked for signs of upset, confusion, anger or any other emotion that became obvious as time passed, while accepting these emotions as normal and trying to help Claire through them.

We do not know everything about adoption and search and reunion, but from our own experience, for what it's worth, if your child is searching or considering it for the future, try and give them your full support in every way possible and be there for them regardless of how it works out. The process takes a long time from start to finish, and love and understanding will be vital for your child's well being. Claire has told us over the years that it helped a lot knowing we were there to listen whenever she needed it and to hold her when things got tough. Just love them and accept them for who they are. Be proud of them. It's not always an easy role, but when you love your child, you will do your best for them.

If we had to try in some small way to offer advice to any adopted person, then that would be to follow your heart, as your feelings are the most important part of this triangle. If you need to search, then go for it. Be true to yourself and, as Claire says, listen to that inner voice.

Eileen, myself, Mary and Claire are only some parts of the puzzle. Aidan is another large part of this process and it is obvious how this has also affected him. The birth mother is another human being, who in many ways, years ago in Ireland, was simply forgotten about. Claire also asked us to offer some advice for any women out there who have had a child adopted. While Mai will obviously be the best person to offer some thoughts and guidance about this, we wish to offer these words. Try to impart as much information as you possibly can to the adoption agency so that contact can be made as easily as possible if after years this child tries to find you.

Once Claire received the initial information and after some letters had passed between them, we always knew that the path to getting to know the gang would be a long, slow one. We found it difficult at times to keep a cool head in trying to slow Claire down. She has always run before she could walk and she has always wanted everything done yesterday. God help your knees or shins if you were watching TV on a Saturday afternoon and she took a fancy to doing some hoovering – she was like a Tasmanian Devil!

We knew, in earlier days, that Rome wouldn't be built in a day and, as Grandad Cashin used to say, 'time heals everything'. We tried to bite our tongues, offering advice where we could without pushing things. Claire found it difficult when Mai needed time before telling her family about her, but as Eileen used say to Claire, 'I can understand Mai's position. As a mum myself with a family of my own, one of the hardest things on earth would be to tell your kids you gave one of them away.' We tried to calm the waters a lot of the time, with what little advice we could offer, but we had to let things take their course. We tried not to push and to always be there to listen.

Like all parents who adopt and love their child, all we wanted was to see Claire fulfilled and happy. To this end, we did our best to understand and support her in every way and help her to find all the answers her heart desired.

We always felt that Claire might search for her birth mother and regardless of the way the search went, we knew that Claire would not love us any less. We are delighted with the way things have worked out and it has definitely made Claire a happier, more complete and confident person.

In all honesty, it never entered our heads that Claire would find both birth parents, and to find that they had married one another was a blessing and the best scenario possible for everyone. It was a bit of a shock when Tony came on the scene, but once we got used to the idea we never felt threatened, as we were always perfectly secure in the love that Claire has for us both.

When searching for some literature to help us explain to Claire about adoption and to find the right words, we read many books. In one such book was the most beautiful verse:

Not flesh of our flesh,
not bone of our bone,
but still miraculously our own.
Never forget for a single minute,
you did not grow under my heart,
but in it.

These words say everything that we have felt for Claire during the years, and I think this verse describes beautifully how adoptive parents feel about their child.

Mary asked that the following words be included, words she read recently that say it all for her too:

As children we had ups and downs,
but the smiles always beat the frowns.
We shared our joys, we shared our dreams,
We shared each other for many years.
You're my sister, you're a treasure,
And my love for you you cannot measure.

19

EVERY STORY SHOULD HAVE A HAPPY ENDING

I'm sure there are times in most everyone's life when you seem so weighed down by confusion, when your thoughts race through your mind at such speed that you feel the pain they cause, yet you seem unable to catch them to understand them, not even for just a second. It's strange the way we are all conditioned in different ways, the way our minds make sense of things when we are ready and not before. For me, it was as if my brain knew when my heart was ready to just open up and feel whatever it had to feel, so that I could begin to figure out how to become whole again, without the doubts or the fear that had been holding me back for years.

Once I allowed myself to give in to these emotions and try to work through them, with the help of both families, I began to actually hear the words people said to me. No more were they just age-old platitudes, but the real meaning in them became clear. 'Time is a great healer' was no longer a saying that annoyed me greatly, because for time to be able to work its magic, you had to use it to think and reason and to figure out what had gone wrong, or, more importantly for me, what had gone right!

And so, I am still learning how to reach a time of deep content-ment and understanding in my life, about myself and of those I love. I have relearned the ability to laugh out loud and smile at the little things in life. I also now, quite regularly, shed a tear, willingly and without shame, knowing it is finally OK to let go of any remaining grief. I've wasted far too many years thinking I wasn't good enough for one stupid reason or another. Believing something so destructive twists your mind and your ability to be all that you're capable of being. I know, without a doubt, that I did not complete this journey on my own. Others in my life taught me that I was not alone and showed me that a time will come when my heart will be at peace. That is what I have found during the past eleven years, in Cork and Wicklow: loved ones who have given me comfort and solace.

The last ten years have passed in what seems like the blink of an eye, and in some of the most challenging years there have been the moments when you know something amazing is happening to you – something so special that it simply takes your breath away. This journey for me, for those I love, is by no means finished, but the hardest times have been and gone.

Mary, my sister, and I were in the bathroom during my thirtieth-birthday celebrations, with a room filled with nearly a hundred people outside, when she looked at me with tears in her eyes. She gave me the most wonderful birthday gift. She held me and said, 'I am so very happy for you and I am glad you have found such happiness and this release.' She told me that whatever makes me happy makes her happy. She had come to terms with the family I had found and had realised that they were not a threat to the love I felt for her. I would love her always, unconditionally, as she had spent thirty years loving me.

That's just it. People are capable of loving passionately and wholeheartedly, in their lives. We have the capacity, if we allow ourselves, to let people into our lives and not to refuse their love because of our own fears, inhibitions or pride. Mary had finally accepted that I would always be her sister and nothing would change that.

When the dust had settled after a number of years, following the initial meeting between Eileen and Colum and Mai, Tony and family, and relationships at long last had begun to flourish, I found myself wondering what would happen between these people. I was the link between two families who, during the normal course of their lives, may not ever have crossed one another's paths. I daydreamed of perhaps a time when Eileen and Mai would call one another to share funny stories or worries within their own lives. Since my first visit to Wicklow, I would have liked nothing better than for Mary to come with me, to let her hair down and enjoy the genuine craic and share the passion they have for life in this part of Ireland. But like most things in life, we all settle into the routine that is most comfortable for us, unwilling at times to venture into situations that might make us feel uncomfortable.

The two families have much in common yet much to tell them apart, and I have a love for each and every family member. It's not so important any more that our lives have not become one, for that was never possible. With so many personalities and individuals with different priorities, I have realised we all have our own lives to lead.

What is important is that I am so lucky, because now I have a family in Wicklow and a family in Cork and each has come to understand that whatever has happened before in my life nothing can change the love that I feel for them all.

When I pop up to Wicklow for a few days every few months or so, as often as I can, Mum and Dad are always first on the phone to me to ask how they all are and to laugh at the shenanigans we got up to while I was there. In Wicklow, I have learned that I just love the thrill of picking up a rifle and aiming and sometimes being able to find the mark, and in time I hope to have a licence and buy my own gun. I think this horrifies Mum and Dad, but they smile and accept it all the same. I am becoming me. In Cork, I share a love of cooking and entertaining with my mum and, perfectionists to the last, we love to get out the good ware and have a shindig, which amuses the gang from Wicklow. They are also learning who

I am, and with this in mind presented me with a beautiful canteen of cutlery on my thirtieth birthday for those special occasions, something that without knowing me well they would not have purchased for me.

After a bout of ill health, Mai and I still have not had the chance to head away for a few days on our own – but all in good time. I know we will make that trip and sooner rather than later. We are learning about one another at the pace both of us are comfortable with. We have spent twenty years apart, and as Mai said recently, during one of my teary episodes on to the phone to her, it hasn't been that long at all in the scheme of things. We snatch weeks or weekends here and there when we can, when our lives will allow us. It's not that we don't want to see one another more often, merely that we all live busy lives and must get to know one another when we can.

Do I love Mai? Yes, a love is growing. Is she just the aunt-type figure she mentioned a while back? She is becoming more to me as time passes. Aidan asked me one drunken night in the wee hours of the morning, 'Who is your favourite?' It's not a question of whom I favour, because I still have much to learn about them all. However, I do seem to have a lot in common with Mai. I seem to know more of the facts and quirks of the rest of the gang, yet Mai and I are so alike in many ways that cannot be denied. It's early days and I look forward to the years ahead.

Despite our earlier misunderstandings, Mai and Tony have managed to show me that their door is always open and that I would always be welcome. Not even that, for the word 'welcome' seems to bestow the status of visitor on me. I walk through their door now and it is natural to switch on the kettle and sit at the kitchen table, as any of them would do. I am becoming truly myself with them and, in doing so, I feel at home there, as much as anywhere else. The fact that I get on so well with the gang, though in part due to their own individual choices, is directly because each of them are a part of Mai and Tony; their personalities, their beliefs and their way of life. They are such special people because of who Mai and Tony are and because of the lessons they have managed to teach their family. And so, I have been blessed because of Mai and Tony. They have made this all possible and because of the open, caring and loving people they are, I have been given a second chance. That gift is precious.

When I visit Wicklow lately, I find myself staying with Joe and Sue, his girlfriend. It allows me to have a few drinks without worrying about driving home, and I tend to sit up after hours and laugh with people I have much in common with, more than just similar DNA. Lisa, now ten, turned to me at home in Wicklow recently and asked me why I don't stay at their home when I visit. I suppose it's harder for the younger ones to understand that it's not from a discomfort at being there – it's just because there are so many people to visit that I have found myself in the routine of staying closer to the watering holes. It's one of the things I love in Wicklow. I am, like them, a night owl and the night usually only gets going after 2 a.m.

Kieran and Lisa have begun to ask some questions about what being adopted means and about my family in Cork. I know by the look on Lisa's face that she does not like the idea of others in Cork who seem to compete for my love. In a child's mind, I guess things are more simple. It's easier for them in many ways to accept, 'Oh, you actually have another sister who lives in Cork.' The progression from being merely a friend of Breda's to being a sister occurred quite naturally for them. They all came down for a quiz night in April 2005, however, and after Mum told Lisa that she loved her and gave her a hug, Lisa whispered in my ear later that she really liked my mum!

Both Lisa and Kieran are teaching me a lot, because until now younger children have not been a part of my life. I have learned that you can't promise them a trip to the swimming pool before a late night and then cancel it because of a hangover. That is a selfish thing to do and it hurts them, so I try to become better at keeping promises. I am amazed at how much they are aware of. When the adults are speaking at the kitchen table in what I consider to be 'code', Kieran is very sharp and knows full well what is going on. They are very special to me, and in time I hope I might be a big sister to them when they need it. Perhaps I might have something to offer too.

My relationship with the rest of the gang, well, we all seem to have found the pace we are comfortable with. I am lucky that the silly and thoughtless manner that I wrote to them two years ago has been forgiven, even by those who hated me for it, for however short a time. I don't like talking on the phone, as I find myself quiet, lost for words at times, and for anyone who knows me this might be hard to believe! So, I don't call them as much as I should, but they have come to accept that and we text jokes and our thoughts for the day every so often or to arrange our next visits. With the arrival of their own children during the past two years, it's not as easy for them to visit Cork, but most of them try and come down this way as often as they can.

Breda and Joe, the closest in age to me, both expressed opinions about a year ago, that they didn't know much about me, that I was difficult to get to know. Old habits die hard, and I am learning to be more open with my beliefs and about who I really am, despite what they might think about me. They know more about me, though, than they realise. They have begun the smart comments about my dependency on lip balm, my giggling when alcohol kicks in, my 'energiser bunny' way when I'm looking after people who stay with us and my joy at being the hostess ... And so much more: my inse-curities, my hopes and the pure elation and joy they have brought to my life. I guess in time we will all learn to ask the right questions, those that will break down any barriers that still exist, those that will bring us closer to one another.

There are times when I make a comment or share an idea with them that I can see a sudden look of interest from one of them, as if they sense an ulterior motive. In some ways, they still do not trust me, and despite never having indicated it, I think they may question if I am pure of heart. All I can do is wait, always be myself and trust that a bond will grow, the sort that will outlast anything. I look forward to that day, I have nothing to hide and don't mind sharing the real me now, faults and all, with those I love.

When I ask questions of them, I can only imagine what they must think, but I hope they know it is not because of a prying need to know what goes on in their lives. I am just trying to get to know them. It was difficult at the start, as they were all so close and protected each other. But learning about each other has begun in quite a natural and unplanned way. I receive telephone calls now in the wee hours of the morning, to tell me to listen to the music being played at a 'Frames' concert they might all be attending. Or they might call me for what seems like just an ordinary chat, only to learn about some secret or to be included in some special news. Since I started writing these words, it has all become so easy – so natural.

I asked Joe a tough question recently, while we shared a 'few' drinks in Kinsale. I asked him did he consider me now to be a friend or a sister, and he answered without hesitation that I was his sister. Aidan laughed and said of course he would say that (because he is a very caring man). But Joe responded that the speed with which he had answered indicated the truth, without having to defend his answer. I cried and he told me to stop being an eejit and we laughed. I believe his words were heartfelt, and I believe he wants me to be his sister, and I am sure I will be in time. Our relationship so far has been a miracle, and they have given me so much more than I ever can give them. But they don't expect anything in return. These people I have been blessed to know and love in Wicklow have become true friends. We met as strangers, as people who knew nothing really about one another, but as time passes we learn about what makes each of us tick. Will I ever really become a sister for them all? I think so, I love them and the truly amazing thing is – I'm not afraid anymore.

We go from strength to strength as the days pass. We visited New York at Easter 2005 with Joe and Sue and Mary Junior, and this was the first time I had the chance to spend more than a day here and there with Mary and we had great craic. Joe and I also had our first barney and, having had far too many drinks, we both said too much, trying to push each other's buttons. But the following day we hugged, laughed at one another's stupidity and knew that the 'honeymoon' stage of our relationship was over. It was now more real, and we begin to really get to know one another now. Like all families, we will hopefully have the sense to give each other some breathing space when it's needed. I believe my mum will also be giving Joe some bridge lessons in the future – it seems she thinks he has an aptitude for it!

I have always been of a 'cuddly' build, and for much of my life I tended to rely on food as a comfort when things got too hard to handle. Quite recently I joined a gym, started swimming and began to lose weight. Dad said something a while back that made a lot of sense to me. He told me that I began to lose weight when the time was right, when I was ready to cast away the hurt, fears and worries and look to the future. I simply had to deal with things before I was ready for this change in my life. It is funny what others can see that you yourself cannot. Mind you, some moments remain when even those closest to you might miss the mark and make an incorrect assumption, despite their best intentions.

Following a recent visit from Joe, Mum turned to me and said, 'I'm glad Joe had a chance to see where you grew up – at least now he can see there is no need to feel sorry for you,' as if the chances and love I had received in life could rid me of all my ghosts.

For any adopted person considering a search in the future, this journey *will not* solve everything, but it might, *just might,* give you the ability to take control of your own life and any insecurities that need to be examined. I am lucky that Eileen and Colum had the emotional stability, honesty and willingness to become truly informed about what the adoption process meant for our family and for me. They have always been prepared, emotionally and psychologically, to meet the needs of their children, adopted or otherwise.

Adoption is a most difficult and complex process for everyone concerned. Adoptees have the right to understand their own feelings, to have them validated and to have access to any information that might help them to heal. I believe that too many adopted people have been made to feel abnormal or a bit crazy when they have been simply responding to feeling abandoned. These past years have not been easy, but no matter how difficult and painful it may have been at times, acknowledging my vulnerabilities and limitations has been crucial to my ability to have more honest and loving relationships with everyone in my life.

Finding the words to finish my story has been hard but I have tried to offer some insight into the peace of mind I have found this past ten years and what I have learned. Writing these words have helped me to learn much about myself. In writing my story I have also had the opportunity to try and help others in similar situations, and that has been the driving force behind this book.

A colleague at work explained something to me recently in very simple English. I had asked him how his work with alternative healing was going and what kind of response it had received in

Cork. He said it was great. He told me that trauma of any sort, or a bad life experience, is like an icon on your computer desktop. Something can happen in life to cause pain and upset, and even though you believe it to be dealt with, it can remain in your life, affecting your sense of self and who you are, the way you react to situations and to others in your life. Like the icon on the computer, the trauma is always sitting there, never quite gone, just waiting to pop up and kick back in again. He said that until all trauma that you might have experienced in life has been seen through to its conclusion, it will stay with you. When it's over, all you're left with is a story, without all the emotion and hurt. I understood what he was saying to me. I think this is that story.

So, the story is told and the lessons have been learned. I've already made mistakes and no doubt have a lot more to make, but I can smile and I can't wait to learn from them. Life is all about making choices and there will be times still, like everyone else in the world, when I make the wrong one. Looking back at the person I was ten years ago, the person I am has not changed much. Sure, I have more confidence and have learned to become more open and honest with myself, less sensitive and angry about the past, but I am still the same person.

All that remains to be said is that if you believe in yourself enough and feel the need to do something in your life, grab any opportunity to truly know yourself with every ounce of your courage and strength. Your choice might not be the easiest one, and chances are you might make a few mistakes along the way, but not everything in life is easy, and sometimes we learn most about ourselves in the hardest times. What a wonderful gift that is!

T. S. Eliot said, 'We shall not cease from exploration. And the end of all our exploring will be to arrive where we started and know the place for the first time.' I am now thirty-two years old and about to *really* start living for the first time in my life, having learned completely who I am. Second chances like this don't come around often, and I'll be damned if I'm going to make the same mistakes twice. I'm going to take each day as it comes and wait for the surprises life has in store for me with a smile on my face ... anything is possible. I am truly blessed.